Perithia, Corfu 11/9/79. G.R.Rant.

CAPSICUM ANNUUM
Sweet Peppers

This Book belongs to:

THE
FRUITS OF THE
EARTH

Vegetable & Fruit Recipes

ADRIAN BAILEY

paintings by Graham Rust

Michael Joseph
London

First published by Michael Joseph Ltd
27 Wrights Lane
London W8
1986

British Library Cataloguing in Publication Data

Bailey, Adrian, *1928–*
    Fruits of the earth: vegetable and fruit recipes.
    1. Cookery (Fruits and Vegetables)
    I. Title   II. Rust, Graham
    641.6′5   TX801

ISBN 0–7181–2737–4

Produced and designed by
Savitri Books Ltd
71 Great Russell Street, London. WC1B 3BN

Art direction and book design: Mrinalini Srivastava
Editor: Myra Street

Typeset in Garamond by Fakenham Photosetting Ltd, Fakenham
Reproduction by Dot Gradations, Chelmsford
Printed and bound in Hong Kong by Mandarin Offset Marketing (H.K.) Ltd

The author wishes to thank Suzanne and Carole Salmon, Leila Kooros,
Alison Scott and Leon Kapikian, for contributing recipes and providing
inspiration.

THE PLATES

Paprika (sweet pepper), *Capsicum frutescens* – half title
French Bean, *Phaseolus vulgaris* – 12
Leek, *Allium porrum* – 19
Pea, *Pisum sativum* – 20
Carrot, *Daucus carota* – 29
Swede, *Brassica napus napobrassica* – 30
Potato, *Solanum tuberosum* – 31
Fennel, *Foeniculum vulgare* – 32
Purple Sprouting Broccoli, *Brassica oleracea botrytis cauliflora* – 41
Egyptian or tree onion, *Allium cepa viviparum* – 42
Tomato, *Lycopersicon esculentum* – 59
Runner Bean, *Phaseolus multiflorus* – 60
Beetroot, *Beta vulgaris* – 69
Chicory (endive), *Cichorium intybus* – 70
Cauliflower, *Brassica oleracea botrytis cauliflora* – 71
Aubergine (eggplant), *Solanum melongena* – 72
Pumpkin, *Cucurbita pepa* – 81
Sweetcorn, *Zea mays* – 82
Savoy Cabbage, *Brassica oleracea capitata* – 99
Onion, *Allium cepa* – 100
Potato, *Solanum tuberosum* – 101
Red Cabbage, *Brassica oleracea capitata* – 102
Brussels Sprout, *Brassica oleracea gemmifera* – 119
Celery, *Apium graviolens dulce* – 120
Celeriac, *Apium graviolens rapacium* – back of jacket
Kitchen garden of Arthington Hall, Yorkshire – front of jacket

INTRODUCTION

This book is a guide to the use of vegetables and fruits prepared in their own right, and to the exploration of their particular qualities. It is a non-vegetarian's consideration of the rewards of vegetable cookery and I have adapted several meat and fish dishes by substituting vegetable or cheese fillings. There is for instance a spicy cabbage recipe where the meat is replaced by aubergines (eggplant), tomatoes, shallots, rice and herbs. Many of the recipes are 'new', inasmuch as any combination of ingredients can be new – there are few, if any, untried combinations, cooking processes or methods for cooks to discover. I have tried to avoid eccentric mixtures for the sake of novelty or to expand the repertoire.

Many dishes will be familiar to readers – they are classics and should be included – others are worthwhile variations on established themes. For example, a *brochette* of marinated, grilled vegetables served with *satay* sauce, or the traditional method of cooking ceps in the Gironde region of France, with parsley and garlic, which can be applied equally well to our fresh field mushrooms. The appeal of a vegetable dish will be greatly enhanced by its presentation and accompaniments: I stress the value of wine, crusty bread and good-quality butter, of freshly-ground pepper, of finely-chopped parsley, herbs, and such simply prepared sauces as *Beurre blanc*, Hollandaise, or the piquant *Rouille*.

I have arranged recipes according to seasons. While many vegetables are now available all the year round, some nevertheless have a prime month in the year when they are at their best, plentiful and therefore a good buy.

In recent years, health considerations have made people aware of the dangers of a diet too high in animal proteins and of the low fibre content in too many processed foods. Vegetarianism has gained increasing numbers of adepts but even for those who do not wish to give up meat, the charm of vegetable cookery has achieved great popularity. This book is therefore aimed at all those, vegetarian or not, who enjoy variety in their diet and who like experimenting with the great wealth of ingredients which swift air freight and the demand generated by ethnic minorities have now made available to the discerning cook, not only in the larger cities of Britain and of the United States, but even in smaller towns.

In Britain, the import of exotic vegetables and fruits has a long history. When Mrs. Beeton published her famous book on *Household Management* in 1861, she was able to advocate the use of sorrel, scorzonera, sweet potatoes, yams, sweetcorn, aubergines (eggplants) and custard apples. It had indeed been possible to buy pineapples, West Indian bananas and American apples on London markets in the eighteenth century. But until fairly recently such items, and of course citrus fruits, were rare and expensive and available only to the privileged few.

Not only the eating but also the cultivation of newly-introduced vegetables and fruits were a privilege of the rich. The seventeenth and eighteenth centuries had witnessed a great interest in the cultivation and propagation of new hybrids. Rich patrons also commissioned artists such as Basil Besler, J. W. Weinmann and Emmanuel Sweert to produce beautiful and detailed botanical paintings and drawings which recorded these developments. Besler's *Hortus Eystettensis* (1613) was sixteen years in the making and occupied six engravers. The two volumes contain some 370 plates, which show each subject life-size, starting with spring flowers and progressing through the year. It had been made for Johann Conrad von Gemmingen, Bishop of Eichstatt, near Nuremberg in Germany, in whose gardens most of the specimens were grown. It is wonderful to see this grand tradition maintained today by such a fine artist as Graham Rust, whose colour plates so admirably illustrate this book.

Today, as a result of the curious economics of modern farming and marketing, one can buy Egyptian potatoes in Bristol that have come via America, and Scottish mushrooms in London that have made their journey via Paris. In my own district of north London I can find fruits and vegetables, some of which I can barely identify. In London's various markets one can buy several varieties of avocado pears, imported from Kenya, Israel and America. There are white aubergines, and the streaked carmine-tinted 'Slim Jims' from Cyprus and Holland, as well as the more familiar, fat and deep purple ones which the resident Greeks use to make moussaka, and which I buy for ratatouille. There are beefsteak tomatoes also from Cyprus, plum tomatoes from Italy and France, but also grown by enterprising English market gardeners.

West Indian, Asian and Chinese shops offer a great variety of fruits and vegetables, some of which are known to their buyers by their Indian or Chinese names only. If you are looking for exotic ingredients, it is better to buy them from ethnic shops, if you have any near you; the high demand for such produce ensures that they are usually fresher than at the local supermarket. Supply varies, of course, depending on where you live but very few are now the places where you cannot find a good selection of unusual ingredients, provided you take the trouble to shop around a little.

Countries like Israel have done a great deal in marketing exotic fruits that do not always travel well over long distances. As the Californian winegrowers who revolutionised their wine production a few years back by planting Riesling and other European vinestocks into their own vineyards, Indian strains of mangoes have been successfully acclimatised by Israeli fruit producers who are able to bring these lovely, fragrant fruits to our table at their peak. Thanks to quick transportation, very good mangoes are now available from India and Pakistan as well as from Mexico and Venezuela. Pineapples from the Ivory Coast, paw-paws from Hawaii, guavas, grapefruit from Cuba – you can even buy coconuts with their outer, shiny-green skin intact around the more familiar fibrous husk.

Cooks are generally conservative by nature. They like a repertoire of tried and tested recipes, using well-known ingredients and processes. Yet despite our natural resistance to the unfamiliar, we are gradually learning to experiment with more unusual vegetables and fruits. Look how that relative newcomer from New Zealand, the kiwi fruit with its lovely colour and unusual tart flavour, has become indispensable to the professional and domestic cook. Until fairly recently, cooks were confounded by the tomato. Was it a fruit or a vegetable? Today the tomato has become as common as the ubiquitous potato. Yet when the latter was first introduced into Europe it was received with mixed reactions: in some parts of France it was supposed to cause leprosy and much later the

French had to be coaxed by Parmentier into eating them – the ill-fated Louis XVI sporting potato flowers in his buttonhole to show his support. Scottish preachers in this country warned their parishioners against eating a product of the soil which was not mentioned in the Bible. Frederick the Great of Prussia had to bully his subjects into liking the potato...

For too long, vegetables were treated as the poor relation, often overcooked, with no effort to bring out their qualities. In many parts of the world, meat is a rarity, but not only on economic grounds as it is often assumed in the West. In countries with a large vegetarian population – usually on religious grounds – dishes are created which are not an apology for lack of meat but are inventive and nutritious. The cookery of India, China and Japan shows a skill and an understanding of vegetables which should serve as a lifelong source of inspiration to western cooks. In this book, however, I have given recipes which follow the European tradition of cooking, although some of the ingredients are exotic.

Vegetables are on the whole delicate and respond best to simple styles of preparation. While red cabbage can be cooked for hours and sauerkraut fermented for days, spinach and spring greens, mange-tout and cauliflower need the briefest heat treatment to bring out their natural flavour and retain their crispness.

9

The Recipes

Read a recipe right through before tackling the actual dish. You may find that some recipes require a long cooking time, or pots and pans with a large capacity. If you do not have a blender or liquidiser, you will have to make allowance for the time-consuming and arduous business of pushing food through a sieve. Check before you cook that you have all the necessary ingredients but do not adopt too narrow an approach to cooking. Most great chefs have 'discovered' new variations on a theme by trial and error. Many an ingredient can be omitted or substituted for another. Cooking times also depend on your preference for 'well-done' or crisper results. In several recipes you will come across a 'medium-sized' onion or tomato. What is medium-sized? It is like specifying quantities of garlic – be guided by your own judgment and taste.

I have not used conventional meat or fish stocks in soups or other dishes. You can add them for extra flavour, if you wish, but if you are a vegetarian you can use a dash of a yeast extract such as Marmite or the vegetable cube stocks which are available from some health food shops. Ready-made pastry containing vegetable fats only is now available from most supermarkets and some brands of Worcestershire sauce do not contain anchovy (check the ingredients).

Be fussy when buying your vegetables or fruits. Do not buy too many at a time as you should use them when they are fresh and crisp. Vegetable dishes, like most other food, are enhanced by presentation and decoration such as chopped parsley, coriander leaves, tomato roses and a fan of gherkins. Many benefit from the addition or use of butter or cream but it is up to you and you can in some cases replace them by yogurt if you are afraid of the high-fat content.

Unless otherwise stated, I tend to use groundnut or safflower oils, or a mixture of the two. Many other polyunsaturates are equally suitable. There is however no real substitute for olive oil and it is important to use it in some salads and in Provençal dishes for authenticity.

Weights & Measures

Ingredients have been specified in **Imperial**, **Metric** and **American** weights and measures. When American terminology differs from the British usage and may cause misunderstandings, the US terms have been included in brackets.

A.B.

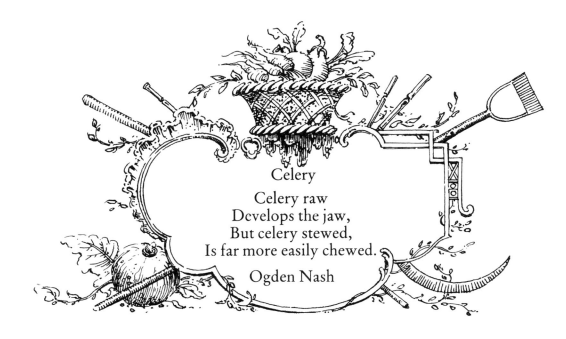

Celery

Celery raw
Develops the jaw,
But celery stewed,
Is far more easily chewed.

Ogden Nash

SPRING

Some years spring can arrive when the ground is still frozen and hard and the last of the snow still lies in sheltered places. Although spring is the season for sowing, not for harvesting, the warmer weather brings the promise of renewed life in the fields and gardens and slowly fresh produce begins to appear on the green-grocers' stalls. The vegetables that we now traditionally associate with spring are new potatoes, new carrots and turnips, spring greens and spring onions. This is a long way from sixteenth-century fare when 'onyans, browne bread, leekes and salt' was all that 'poore men could daily gnaw'. Springtime was the period of the 'hungry gap' during Lent when the 'hungry gap kale' and the swede turnip came into their own. Then and now, however, leeks are part of the St. David's Day celebrations in Wales.

CRÈME ST. GERMAIN

Makes four servings.

	Imperial	Metric	American
Spring onions (scallions) or small onions – 4			
Lettuce heart – 1			
Butter	1 oz	30 g	2 tbsp
Shelled peas	1 lb	450 g	3 cups
Mint – 1 sprig			
Plain (all purpose) flour	2 oz	55 g	½ cup
Milk approx.	½ pint	300 ml	1¼ cups
Salt and pepper			
Single (coffee) cream	5 fl oz	150 ml	⅔ cup
Petit pois	4 oz	115 g	¼ lb

Finely chop onions, shred the lettuce and sweat over a gentle flame in half the heated butter. Add the shelled peas and the mint. The best flavour comes from peas at the peak of their season – you can, of course, substitute frozen peas, but with the inevitable loss of flavour. The *petit pois* are used as a garnish.

Add a little water to the pan containing the peas and onions, and stew gently for about 10 minutes, adding more liquid if needed. Press the peas through a sieve, or puree in a blender.

Make a roux with the remaining butter and flour, thinning down with enough milk to make a sauce (you will need about ½ pint/300 ml/1¼ cups).

Mix with the pea puree, then season to taste, thinning with extra milk if needed. Add the cream, then stir in the *petit pois*. Serve hot with French bread or croûtons.

MANGE-TOUT SOUP

You can make this soup with young pea pods, or when mange-tout (edible-podded) peas are cheap, or rather, relatively cheap.

Makes four servings.

	Imperial	Metric	American
Butter (for frying)	1 oz	30 g	2 tbsp
Mange-tout (edible-podded) peas or young pea pods	8 oz	225 g	½ lb
Medium-sized onion – 1			
Sprig of mint – 1			
Water	1¾ pints	1 litre	1 quart
Lettuce – 1			
Butter for roux	1 oz	30 g	2 tbsp
Plain (all purpose) flour	1 tbsp	1 tbsp	1 tbsp
Sugar	1 level tsp	1 level tsp	1 level tsp
Salt and pepper			

Chop and sauté the onion in butter until soft. Break up pods with your fingers, wash and drain. Add to the onion and stir-fry for 1 minute, then add outer leaves of the lettuce, well-washed (you can, if you like, include the entire lettuce, or leave the heart for salad). Also add mint and sugar. Boil for 20 minutes or until pods are soft. Puree in a liquidiser. Press the soup through a sieve – if you don't do this, stringy fibres will remain in the soup.

Make a roux by melting butter and adding the flour, stir, and gradually add the soup to thicken. The soup is improved by the addition of a little cream or even milk. Season to taste, and serve with croûtons.

PETITE ENTREE DU JARDIN

Makes four servings.

	Imperial	Metric	American
Young carrots – 6			
Mushrooms	4 oz	115 g	1 cup
Spring onions (scallions) – small bunch			
Cauliflower – half			
Oil	3 tbsp	3 tbsp	Scant ¼ cup
Garlic – one clove			
Eggs – 2			
Milk and cream mixture, half and half	8 fl oz	225 ml	1 cup
Nutmeg – a pinch			
Salt and pepper			

Preheat oven to 180°C/350°F/Gas Mark 4.

Scrape carrots, slice, then chop finely. Slice and chop mushrooms. Break cauliflower into tiny flowerets, finely slice spring onions. Stir-fry the vegetables in oil with a crushed clove of garlic, salt and pepper.

Beat the eggs with the cream, add a grating of nutmeg. Put a heaped table-spoonful of vegetables, when cooked *al dente*, into individual ramekins, or heatproof bowls, and add a measure of the cream to cover. Put the dishes in a bain-marie, and bake in the oven for about 20 minutes or until the centre is just firm.

This dish can be eaten hot or cold. You can vary the balance of vegetables, and the quantities and types, depending on the season, but the dish should be composed of fresh, finely-chopped and blended vegetables, rather undercooked than overdone.

BRIE AND SPINACH IN PASTRY

This makes a pleasant if rather challenging first course; the challenge is to serve the portions before the melted cheese escapes from the pastry case (pie shell). The spinach blends with the brie during the cooking. Quantities can, of course, be varied according to the number of guests to be served.

Makes four servings.

	Imperial	Metric	American
A wedge of brie cheese, firm and not overripe	8 oz	225 g	½ lb
Pureed spinach approx.	2–3 oz	55–85 g	¼–⅓ cup
Small package frozen puff pastry	7 oz	200 g	7 oz
Egg wash or milk			

Take the wedge of cheese and slice it across, so that you have two thin wedges of cheese; then place them together to form a rectangle.

Roll out the pastry to make a rectangle 10″ × 17″ (25 cm × 43 cm) and place the cheese in the centre.

Cover with a layer of spinach, brush edges of pastry with a wet brush, fold over the top and press edges to make a firm seal, pinch edges or press with the prongs of a fork. Brush pastry with egg wash or milk and leave for 1 hour to rest in a cool place.

Preheat oven to 200° C/425° F/Gas Mark 7.

Bake pastry until well risen (about 10 to 15 minutes).

This goes very well with an Alsace wine, such as a Gewürztraminer.

STUFFED ARTICHOKE BOTTOMS WITH AVOCADO

Makes four servings.

	Imperial	Metric	American
Artichokes – 4			
Salt			
Avocado pear – 1			
Garlic clove, minced – 1			
Tomato puree or dried tomato paste	1 tsp	1 tsp	1 tsp
Mayonnaise, see page 67	2 tbsp	2 tbsp	3 tbsp
Lemon juice	1 tsp	1 tsp	1 tsp
Pepper			
Parsley – 4 small sprigs			

Cut artichoke stems flush to bottoms of the leaves. Put heads in a large pan of boiling, salted water and simmer for 30 minutes, or until a base leaf pulls away easily.

Drain, cool, then pull leaves away. With a sharp knife scrape the edible pulp away from the base of each leaf. Scoop pulp into a small bowl. Remove the fibrous 'choke' carefully, and trim the remaining base neatly.

Take the avocado, ripe but not too soft, and cut across the centre – not lengthwise – to the stone. Twist the two halves and remove stone. Cut pear into rings about ¼″ (50 mm) to ⅜″ (75 mm) thick, peel away skin.

Surplus ends of pear are to be added to the artichoke pulp in the bowl and mashed until smooth, with the minced garlic, tomato paste, the mayonnaise, a squeeze of lemon and pepper.

Put 1 artichoke bottom on each circle of avocado pear, fill with as much of the puree as the artichokes will take without spilling over. Decorate with a tiny sprig of parsley. Chill before serving.

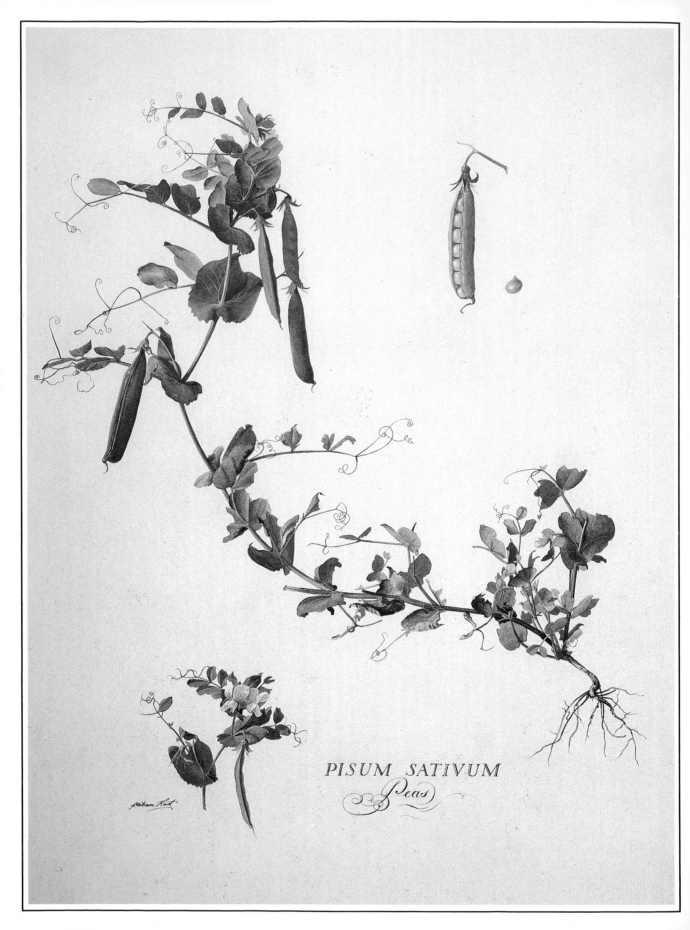

PISUM SATIVUM

Peas

SPRING VEGETABLES WITH PASTA

You can use any suitable assortment of fresh vegetables, according to the supply: mange-tout edible-podded peas, new broad (fava) beans, peas, courgettes, sliced custard marrow (patty pan squash), celery, young carrots, and so on. Use fresh pasta if you can get it; many Italian shops and even supermarkets now sell fresh pasta, such as tagliatelli, *and* paglia e fieno, *the green and yellow of the latter making an attractive dish.*

Makes four servings as a starter and two servings as a main course.

	Imperial	Metric	American
Mixed vegetables	8 oz	225 g	½ lb
Oil	1 tbsp	1 tbsp	1 tbsp
Mixed herbs	1–2 tsp	1–2 tsp	1–2 tsp
Garlic – 1 clove			
Sugar	1 tsp	1 tsp	1 tsp
Salt and pepper			
Pasta	8 oz	225 g	½ lb
Cream	2–3 tbsp	2–3 tbsp	3–4 tbsp
Butter	2 oz	55 g	¼ cup

Chop vegetables fairly fine, but so that they retain their identity, and blanch them in boiling water for 2 minutes. Now sauté them in oil, with a sprinkling of finely-chopped herbs, such as basil, oregano, chervil and parsley, minced garlic, sugar and salt and pepper to taste – 5 minutes cooking should be sufficient, so that they remain crispy, or *al dente*.

Cook the pasta, drain and toss with the cream. Similarly, toss the vegetables in the butter and add to the pasta. Stir and serve, with grated parmesan cheese if liked.

AUBERGINE PATE

This pâté *is made in Provence, and is related to the* Petite entrée du jardin *on page 16 as it has a flan base of milk and eggs.*
Makes eight servings.

	Imperial	Metric	American
Aubergines (eggplant), large	1½ lb	680 g	1½ lb
Garlic clove – 1			
Eggs – 4			
Milk, approx.	1 pint	600 ml	2½ cups
Fresh brown breadcrumbs	2 oz	55 g	1 cup
Mixed herbs	1 tsp	1 tsp	1 tsp
Salt and black pepper	2–3 tsp	2–3 tsp	2–3 tsp
Oil	6 fl oz	175 ml	¾ cup

Slice and finely chop the aubergines (eggplant), and sauté in oil until lightly brown – you will need at least 8 tablespoonfuls of oil, and you will have to stir-fry the aubergines (eggplant) in batches. Put them in a bowl as you finish cooking.

To the final batch add the garlic, finely-chopped, and the herbs. Mix the aubergines (eggplant) and other ingredients together.

Beat the eggs with the milk, add salt and pepper. Pour onto the aubergines (eggplant) and stir in the breadcrumbs. Bake in an ovenproof terrine dish, or a long loaf tin, at 180° C/350° F/Gas 4 for 30 minutes. Lower the temperature to 150° C/300° F/Gas 2 and cook for a further 50 minutes, or until the mixture has completely set. Leave to cool.

To serve, cut into slices, arranged to overlap on a serving dish and decorate with chopped parsley. A TOMATO COULIS (page 23) often accompanies this pâté, with green salad and French bread.

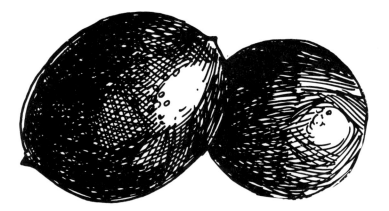

TOMATO COULIS

Makes four servings.

	Imperial	Metric	American
Medium-sized onion – 1			
Oil	1½ tbsp	1½ tbsp	2 tbsp
Tomatoes, fresh or	1 lb	400 g	1 lb
canned	1 (14 oz)	1 (400 g)	1 (14 oz)
Oregano	¼ tsp	¼ tsp	¼ tsp
Sugar	1 tsp	1 tsp	1 tsp
Salt and pepper			

Chop the onion finely and sauté in a little oil until soft. Add the tomatoes, skinned and chopped if fresh, or if canned, include the juice. Add the oregano, sugar, salt and pepper to taste. Simmer for 10 minutes uncovered, or until the tomatoes are soft, then pass through a sieve or puree in a blender. Serve hot or cold.

ONION TART

To make 1 × 9″ (23 cm) tart (pie shell).

FOR THE PASTRY

	Imperial	Metric	American
Plain (all purpose) flour	6 oz	170 g	1½ cups
Butter, chilled	4 oz	115 g	½ cup
Egg yolk – 1			
Iced water	3 tbsp	3 tbsp	Scant ¼ cup

FOR THE FILLING

	Imperial	Metric	American
Onions	1 lb	450 g	1 lb
Butter	1 oz	30 g	2 tbsp
Oil	2 tbsp	2 tbsp	3 tbsp
Eggs – 3			
Mixture of cream and milk, about half and half	10 fl oz	275 ml	1¼ cups
Salt and pepper			
Nutmeg			

Sieve the flour into a bowl.

Work the butter finely into the flour to the texture of breadcrumbs. Add egg yolk mixed with the water, mix to make a dough and leave to rest. Roll out pastry to fill a 9″ (23 cm) tart (pie shell) dish – the thinner the pastry the better.

Allow to rest in the refrigerator.

Preheat oven to 180° C/350° F/Gas Mark 4.

Meanwhile, finely slice the onions and sauté in the remaining butter heated with about 2 tablespoons of oil. Cook over a very low heat until soft and translucent, then drain off the fat.

In a mixing bowl put 1 whole egg plus 2 yolks and beat with the cream/milk mixture. Add 1 level teaspoon of salt, pepper, nutmeg, and the onions. Pour into the unbaked pastry case (pie shell) and bake on centre shelf for 25–30 minutes, or until just set in the centre.

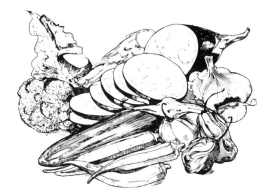

LEEK AND POTATO QUICHE

To make 1 × 8″ (20 cm) flan.

	Imperial	Metric	American
Pastry recipe see page 24			
Potatoes	1 lb	450 g	1 lb
Garlic – 1 clove			
Bay leaf – 1			
Leeks – 3 or 4			
Butter	1 oz	30 g	2 tbsp
Eggs – 3			
Equal mixture of cream and milk	10 fl oz	275 ml	1¼ cups
Salt and pepper			
Nutmeg			

Use the pastry recipe for onion tart (page 24) and roll out very thinly to line the tart dish (pie shell). Leave to rest in the refrigerator while you make the filling. Peel the potatoes and slice them evenly to ⅛″ (25 mm) thickness. Put them to boil with the clove of garlic and the bay leaf until they are half cooked, about 5 minutes at the most. Drain and plunge into cold water, drain thoroughly. Sauté the leeks in the butter until soft. It may help, after about 7 minutes sautéing, to add a little water to soften the leeks. When they are ready, leave to cool.

Preheat the oven to 190° C/375° F/Gas Mark 5.

Beat the eggs with the milk/cream mixture, season well with salt and pepper. Spread the leeks on the bottom of the pastry case (pie shell), pour a little of the egg mixture over them, then a layer of potatoes. Fill the case with egg mixture and potatoes alternately. Grate a little nutmeg on top and bake for about 25 minutes, or until nicely browned on top. Serve warm, with a crisp green salad.

KOULABIAK WITH AUBERGINES, MUSHROOMS AND CREAM CHEESE

The inspiration for this perfect luncheon dish came originally from the classic koulabiak – puff pastry surrounding a filling of sturgeon and rice. Instead of the fish, I have substituted a cream cheese. I used a tub of French Tartine, but Boursin could be used. The filling is alternate layers of saffron rice with a mirepoix of vegetables, cheese and fresh herbs.

Makes four to six servings.

	Imperial	Metric	American
Puff pastry – frozen or home made	13 oz	370 g	13 oz
Cream cheese – French Tartine or Boursin	8 oz	225 g	½ lb
Long grain rice	5 oz	140 g	¾ cup
Packet powdered saffron – 1			
Medium-sized aubergine (eggplant) – 1			
Shallots – 2 or 3			
or medium-sized onion – 1			
Mushrooms	6 oz	170 g	1½–2 cups
Eggs, hard-boiled (cooked) – 2			
Egg yolk – 1			
Butter	4 oz	115 g	½ cup
Fresh parsley – several sprigs			
Fresh dill – several sprigs			
Salt and black pepper			

Allow time for pastry to defrost if using frozen pastry. Boil aubergine (eggplant) for 15 minutes. Hard boil (cook) the 2 eggs. Cook rice in ½ pint/300 ml/1¼ cups of water with the saffron and a pinch of salt. Cover the pan once the water boils, and cook on the lowest possible flame for 20 minutes. Turn onto a dish and leave to cool.

Meanwhile, chop shallots finely, sauté in half the heated butter. Peel and chop the aubergine, chop mushrooms and sauté both with the shallots, adding a little oil if needed. Season with salt and pepper. Set aside to cool. Finely chop the eggs, parsley and dill, mix well and set aside.

Roll out the pastry on a well-floured board to a rectangle about 15″ × 12″ (37 × 30 cm). Trim off a ¼″ (50 mm) strip all round and set aside. Brush centre of pastry with melted butter. Spread a layer of rice lengthways along the pastry, cover with a layer of sautéed vegetables, with some of the egg, then a layer of all the cheese. Cover with a further layer of egg, vegetables and rice. Melt remaining butter and pour over filling.

Wet edges of the pastry, bring edges together to form a sausage shape, fold to form a central seam, pinching edges firmly to seal. Seal ends likewise – if you have too much pastry, trim off surplus. Turn over and mould with hands to a neat, compact shape, tucking in the ends.

Decorate with strips to form a lattice. Brush with egg yolk and refrigerate for at least 1 hour.

Preheat the oven to 200° C/400° F/Gas Mark 6. Bake the pastry on centre shelf until nicely browned – about 25 minutes. Leave to cool before serving – the *koulabiak* should be warm but not hot. Serve with a *beurre blanc* sauce (page 40) and a salad.

BRAISED LEEKS OR ENDIVE, WITH OLIVES AND GARLIC

Makes four servings.

	Imperial	Metric	American
Leeks – 8			
Butter	1 oz	30 g	2 tbsp
Fat garlic cloves – 5 or 6			
Green olives – 16–20			
Oregano			
Salt and pepper			
Croûtons of fried bread			

Preheat oven to 160° C/325° F/Gas Mark 3.

If you use endive – the white *witloof*, also known as chicory, and not the curly endive – blanch in boiling water for 5 minutes, then drain.

Leeks should be well washed, and trimmed just where the white turns to green. Slice the leeks lengthways, likewise the endives, and put them in an oven dish with a lid. Add the butter, the oregano, the peeled cloves of garlic, and the olives. Season with salt and pepper, and braise in the oven for 1 hour, basting from time to time. The leeks will have turned brown, the garlic soft.

To serve, allow 2 leeks per person, and a few olives. Spread the garlic on croûtons, to accompany the leeks.

VEGETABLE PATE

A pleasantly coarse, moist pâté *made with lentils and vegetables.*
Makes six servings.

	Imperial	Metric	American
Brown or French grey lentils	3 oz	85 g	Generous ⅓ cup
Shallots – 2			
Garlic clove – 1			
Large aubergine (eggplant)	12 oz	350 g	¾ lb
Mushrooms	4 oz	115 g	1 cup
Courgettes (zucchini)	8 oz	225 g	½ lb
Oil	2 fl oz	55 ml	¼ cup
Oregano	1 tsp	1 tsp	1 tsp
Salt and pepper			
Cream cheese, such as Philadelphia	3 oz	85 g	3 oz
Egg yolk – 1			
Chopped parsley			
Gherkins			
Olives			
French bread			

Soak lentils for 1 hour, then simmer in water to cover (about 1 pint/600 ml/2½ cups) until soft. Drain and leave to cool.

Meanwhile, finely chop the vegetables. Sauté the shallot first then the garlic clove. Add the aubergine (eggplant), mushrooms and courgettes (zucchini). Stir in the oregano and season to taste with salt and pepper.

Preheat oven to 180° C/350° F/Gas Mark 4.

In a bowl, mix the sautéed vegetables with the lentils, the cheese, and the egg yolk, well mashed together. Put in a small terrine, or ovenproof dish with a lid, and bake for 45 minutes to 1 hour. The pâté will be browned around the edges.

When cold, cut into slices. Sprinkle with chopped parsley, serve with sliced gherkins, olives, and French bread.

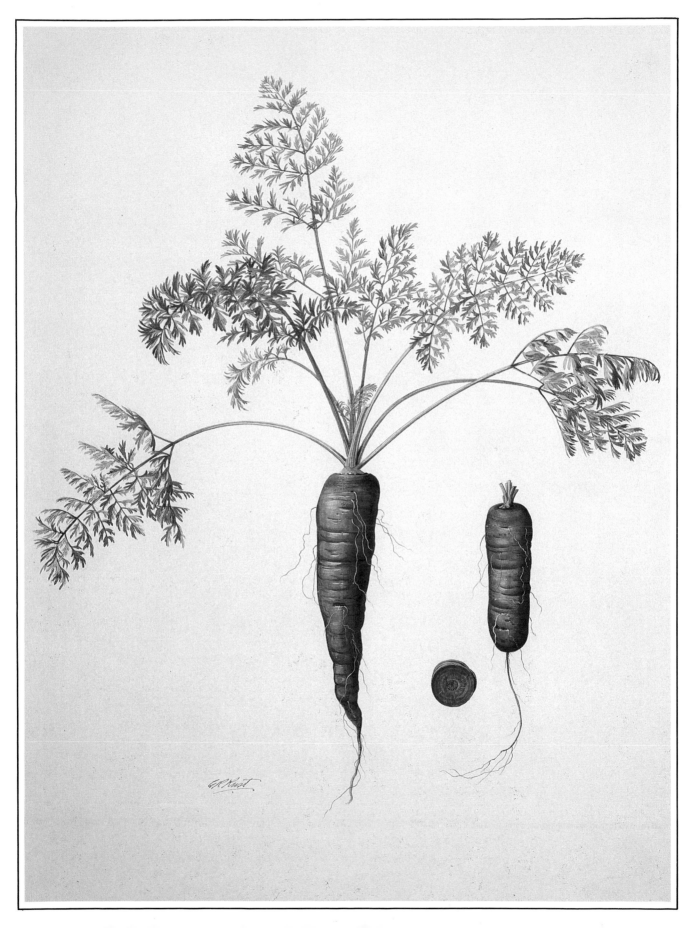

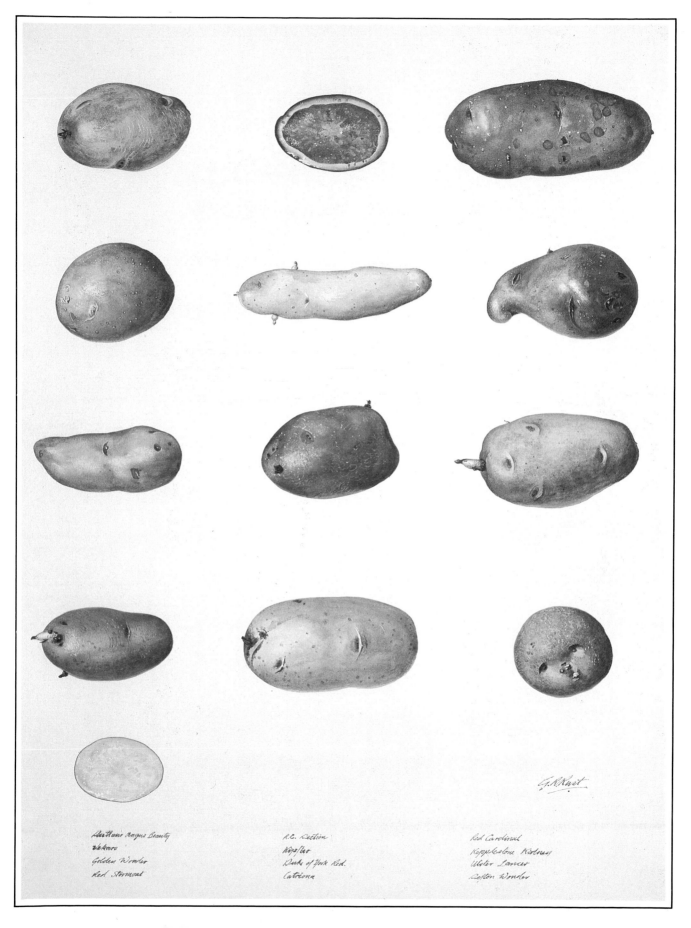

Hartlers Angus Beauty

Nehroo

Golden Wonder

Red Stormont

R.C. Railton

Röpsler

Duke of York Red.

Catriona

Red Cardinal

Kepplestone Kidney

Ulster Lancer

Arran Wonder

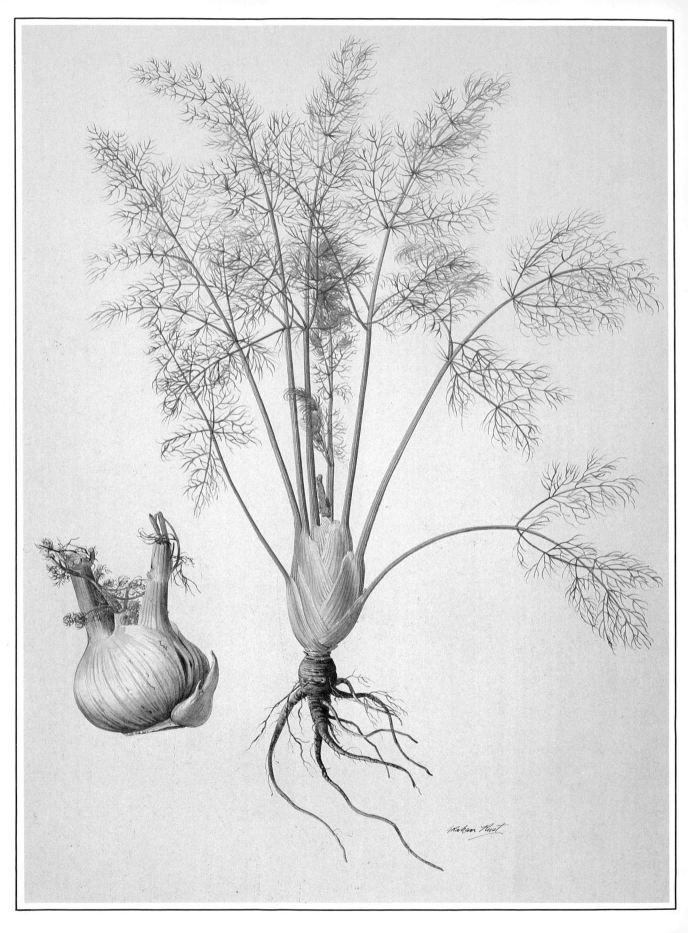

SALAD OF NEW POTATOES AND HERBS

This dish can be eaten hot, as an accompaniment to a main dish, or eaten cold as a salad. On the other hand, it could almost be served as a meal in itself.

Makes six servings.

	Imperial	Metric	American
Potatoes	2 lb	1 kg	2 lb
Bouquet garni – 1			
Garlic – 2 cloves			
Parsley – several sprigs			
Coriander – 1 sprig			
Tarragon – 1 sprig			
Mint – several leaves			
Basil leaves – a few			
Olive oil	4 tbsp	4 tbsp	5 tbsp
Lemon juice	1 tbsp	1 tbsp	1 tbsp
Salt and pepper			
Egg yolk, optional – 1			

Scrub or scrape the potatoes or, if you prefer, leave their skins intact but wash well. Boil until tender in a bouillon with bouquet garni and garlic added.

While they are cooking, chop some fresh parsley, fresh coriander, tarragon, mint and basil, or whatever fresh herbs are available – the parsley, though, is essential.

Drain the potatoes, add the herbs, and toss in a dressing of good olive oil, lemon juice, salt and black pepper. You can also add an optional egg yolk as an emollient.

LENTIL SALAD

A spicy compote *of lentils and onion, flavoured with mint.*
Makes six servings.

	Imperial	Metric	American
Brown lentils	1 lb	450 g	1 lb
Medium-sized onion – 1			
Salt and black pepper			
Cloves – 2			
Cumin seeds	1 heaped tsp	1 heaped tsp	1 heaped tsp
Fresh mint – 1 handful			
Olive oil	1 tbsp	1 tbsp	1 tbsp
Sugar	1 tsp	1 tsp	1 tsp
Dry mustard powder	1 tsp	1 tsp	1 tsp
Dash of wine vinegar			

Wash lentils thoroughly, removing any small stones. Drain well. Chop the onion finely and sprinkle with salt, black pepper and pounded cloves (or use powdered cloves). Combine with the lentils, add the cumin seeds (also pounded) and stir until well mixed. Cover with water, leave overnight or for at least 6 hours.

Boil lentils over a gentle heat until they are just cooked. Top up the water during cooking if necessary. Strain, leave to cool, and refrigerate until cold.

Chop up most of the mint, add to the lentils with the oil, vinegar, sugar and mustard. Stir thoroughly and serve with a little fresh mint on top.

ORANGE AND ALMOND TART

This is a fairly quick and easy one to make, if you have the ingredients to hand – a packet of trifle sponges, oranges and some ground almonds.

First make a pastry case (pie shell) as for pear and almond tart on page 90. Then make the filling as follows:

Makes six to eight servings.

	Imperial	Metric	American
Juice of 2 medium-sized oranges			
Castor (fine granulated) sugar	4 oz	115 g	½ cup
Grated rind of 1 orange			
Ground almonds	3 oz	85 g	¾ cup
Eggs – 2			
Trifle sponges – 1 × pack of 8			
Double (whipping) cream to serve			

Preheat oven to 180° C/350° F/Gas Mark 5.

Beat the sugar in the orange juice, add the grated rind, almonds, the eggs well beaten, and the sponges reduced to crumbs. This takes a matter of seconds in an electric mixer. Pour the batter in the pastry case (pie shell) and bake for 20 minutes, or until a skewer inserted in the middle comes out clean. Glaze with a syrup made from 1 tablespoonful of water and 1 of sugar boiled for 1 minute. Eat the tart warm, with cream.

PAPAYA AND LIME MOUSSE

This dish is a light mousse set in a ring of sponge fingers, with the unusual flavour of papaya, or paw-paw – the brilliant orange-coloured fruit with the seeds that look like large caviar, and taste like nasturtium leaves. The sponge fingers are not essential – you can serve the mousse plain. The quantities given here are for a straight-sided soufflé dish, or similar container, 7" × 3" (18 cm × 7.5 cm) and a 12" × 10" (30 cm × 25 cm) tin for the sponges.

Makes six to eight servings.

FOR THE SPONGE

	Imperial	Metric	American
Eggs – 3			
Castor (fine granulated) sugar	3 oz	85 g	⅓ cup
Plain (all purpose) flour	3 oz	85 g	¾ cup

FOR THE MOUSSE

	Imperial	Metric	American
Papaya – 1			
Limes – 3			
Castor (fine granulated) sugar	8 oz	225 g	1 cup
Eggs – 4			
Cornflour (cornstarch)	2 tsp	2 tsp	2 tsp
Gelatine – 1 sachet (envelope) (Davis's gelatine)	5 level tsp	5 level tsp	5 level tsp
Single (coffee) cream	5 oz	150 ml	⅔ cup

Preheat oven to 180° C/350° F/Gas Mark 4.

Separate the eggs, cream yolks with the sugar until light and fluffy. Whip whites to a stiff froth, fold into the egg mixture, alternatively with the flour. Pour this batter onto a well-greased baking sheet, and bake for 7 minutes on the middle shelf. Leave to cool.

Now cut the papaya in half, remove the seeds. Spoon pulp into a blender with the juice of the limes, add the sugar, and yolks of the eggs, reserving the whites. Add the cornflour (cornstarch), and blend at top speed – it should yield about ½ pint/300 ml/1¼ cups of pulp. If you don't possess a blender, press the pulp through a sieve, beat with the lime juice and remaining ingredients. Put in a pan and boil for 2 minutes, stirring as it thickens.

Dissolve the gelatine in 4 fl oz/115 ml/½ cup of hot water. Add gelatine to the mixture, then stir in the cream. Whip egg whites stiff, and fold in.

Cut a circle of greaseproof (wax) paper to fit the bottom of your soufflé dish. Butter it, and the sides of the dish thoroughly. Cut sponge fingers, about 1" (2½ cm) wide, to fit around the sides of the dish. Pour in the mousse and leave to set – at least 4 hours. Trim tops of sponge fingers if they are standing proud of the dish's rim.

To serve, slip a knife around the sponge, and carefully invert onto a serving dish. Peel the paper away.

BANANAS IN RED WINE

Makes two servings.

	Imperial	Metric	American
Red wine	5 fl oz	140 ml	⅔ cup
Sugar	2 oz	55 g	¼ cup
Cinnamon	½ tsp	½ tsp	½ tsp
Bananas – 2			
Lemon juice	1 tsp	1 tsp	1 tsp

Put the wine in a small pan with the sugar and cinnamon. Bring to the boil, boil for 2 minutes, then add the bananas, peeled and sliced lengthwise. Cook until the sauce is syrupy and the bananas are soft. Turn into a serving dish, and squeeze a little lemon juice over them. Serve warm, with cream.

DUTCH APPLE FRITTERS

Cinnamon-flavoured apple rings in beer batter.
  Makes four servings.

	Imperial	Metric	American
Bread (strong white) or plain (all purpose) flour	4 oz	115 g	1 cup
Castor (fine granulated) sugar	2 tsp	2 tsp	2 tsp
Small can of lager beer – 1			
Granny Smith or other firm dessert apples – 4			
Cinnamon	1 tsp	1 tsp	1 tsp
Oil for frying	¾ pint	425 ml	2 cups
Icing (confectioner's) sugar	2 tbsp	2 tbsp	3 tbsp

Put the flour and sugar in a mixing bowl. Gradually add the beer, to make a smooth batter. If you use bread (strong white) flour, it will absorb about ¾ of the can to get to the right consistency, and slightly less if you use plain (all purpose) flour. To drink the remainder is the cook's privilege!

Peel and core the apples and cut across in slices ¼" (50 mm) thick. Sprinkle with cinnamon. You will need about ¾ pint/425 ml/scant 2 cups of light cooking oil in a deep, heavy pan unless, of course, you have an automatic fryer. Dip each apple ring in the batter, let the surplus run off, and fry 3 or 4 at a time until golden. Drain on absorbent paper. Dredge with icing sugar before serving.

PASHA

A traditional Russian Easter fruit and cheese cake, served with apricot sauce, and the spiced bread called Kulich.

Makes six servings.

	Imperial	Metric	American
Soft but dry cream cheese	4 oz	115 g	¼ lb
Butter	2 oz	55 g	¼ cup
Castor (fine granulated) sugar	2 oz	55 g	¼ cup
Ground almonds	1 oz	30 g	¼ cup
Seedless raisins	4 oz	115 g	⅔ cup
Candied orange peel	2 oz	55 g	⅓ cup
Cultured sour cream	3 tbsp	3 tbsp	Scant ¼ cup

Press the cheese through a sieve. Cream the butter and sugar until light and fluffy. Add the ground almonds, raisins, finely-chopped candied peel, soured cream and the cream cheese. Mix thoroughly.

Line a mould with a muslin cloth – you can use a flowerpot, to achieve something approaching the traditional fez shape – and spoon the mixture into it. Fold the cloth over the top, and cover with a weight to press the mixture down.

Put the Pasha in a cool place and leave for at least 12 hours. Invert onto a serving dish, removing the muslin. Serve with an APRICOT SAUCE:

	Imperial	Metric	American
Dried apricots	3 oz	100 g	½ cup
Sugar	1 heaped tbsp	1 heaped tbsp	1 heaped tbsp
Lemon rind			

Soak the apricots overnight. Put in a pan with water to cover the fruit, add the sugar and a thin strip of lemon rind. Simmer until the apricots are soft, allow to cool slightly then puree in a blender or pass through a sieve. If the sauce is too thick, add a little water. Serve cold.

BEURRE BLANC

A classic butter sauce from the Loire region of France, and also from Brittany. The Bretons used a great deal of butter in their cooking: fresh farmhouse butter, rich in lactose and whey. These constituents helped to emulsify the sauce, and it is difficult to make a true beurre blanc *with modern, refined butters.*

The sauce is made on the principle of mayonnaise, using a puree of shallots to start the emulsifying process. My version short-cuts the problems involved by using an egg yolk. The preparation is made even easier if you have a blender.

To make approximately 5 fl oz/150 ml/⅔ cup.

	Imperial	Metric	American
Shallot – 1			
Tarragon vinegar	1 tbsp	1 tbsp	1 tbsp
Water	3 tbsp	3 tbsp	Scant ¼ cup
Melted butter	2 oz	55 g	¼ cup
Softened butter	3 oz	85 g	⅓ cup
Egg yolk – 1			

Finely chop a shallot. Boil in a pan with tarragon vinegar and water until the liquid has almost evaporated. Warm your mixing bowl, and have ready both the melted and the softened butter. Tip the shallot into the bowl, add 1 egg yolk and whisk at top speed, adding the melted butter very slowly. As the sauce thickens, add softened butter by degrees.

Serve immediately, for if the butter gets cold, it hardens and cannot easily be reconstituted.

BECHAMEL SAUCE

Perhaps the most familiar of all sauces. It is a basic white sauce, a roux made with equal amounts of butter and flour, thinned with cold milk, and flavoured with nutmeg. You may add lemon juice to sharpen it, and cream or egg yolk – or both – to make it richer.

To make approximately 1 pint/600 ml/2½ cups.

	Imperial	Metric	American
Butter	2 oz	55 g	¼ cup
Plain (all purpose) flour	2 oz	55 g	½ cup
Milk (depending on the thickness required)	¾–1 pint	425 ml–600 ml	2–2½ cups
Nutmeg – 1 pinch			
Salt and pepper			
Lemon juice ⎫	1 tsp	1 tsp	1 tsp
Cream ⎬ optional	2–3 tbsp	2–3 tbsp	3–4 tbsp
Egg yolk – 1 ⎭			

Melt the butter and stir in the flour, then gradually add milk, stirring con-

tinuously to avoid lumps forming. Season with salt and pepper and flavour with a little grated nutmeg.

Add paprika and you have an AURORE SAUCE. If you want a MORNAY SAUCE, for cauliflower cheese for example, add Parmesan cheese, or grated Gruyère, or both.

BEARNAISE SAUCE

Makes ¾ pint/425 ml/scant 2 cups.

	Imperial	Metric	American
Dry white wine	4 fl oz	115 ml	½ cup
Shallots, finely chopped – 2			
Peppercorns – 10			
Bay leaf – 1			
Bouquet garni of tarragon, chervil, thyme and parsley – 1 sachet or 1 fresh bunch			
Egg yolks – 5			
Butter	5 oz	140 g	⅔ cup
Salt – 1 pinch			
Tarragon – 1 sprig			
Parsley – a few sprigs			

Boil the wine with the shallots and herbs until reduced to 2 tablespoons of liquid. Leave to cool. Beat the egg yolks in a bowl, and strain the cooled herb/wine mixture over them.

Cook in a bain-marie or double-boiler over a gentle heat until the sauce begins to thicken. Add the butter by degrees stirring continuously, but watch it doesn't curdle. Season with salt, then add fresh chopped tarragon and parsley.

Mint substituted for tarragon will give you a PALOISE SAUCE. Add a squeeze of tomato paste to the basic *Béarnaise*, and you have a CHORON SAUCE.

HOLLANDAISE SAUCE

Similar to Béarnaise *(page 43), but prepared with vinegar and sharpened with lemon juice.*

Makes approximately ¾ pint/425 ml/scant 2 pints.

	Imperial	Metric	American
White wine or tarragon vinegar	4 fl oz	125 ml	½ cup
Shallots, finely chopped – 2			
Butter	5 oz	150 g	⅔ cup
Egg yolks – 6			
Peppercorns – 10			
Bay leaf – 1			
Salt – 1 pinch			
Lemon juice	1 tbsp	1 tbsp	1 tbsp

Reduce the vinegar with the herbs to 2 tablespoons liquid. Beat eggs in a bowl, and strain the cooled vinegar over them. Stir in a bain-marie, and proceed as for *Béarnaise* (page 43), adding the butter gradually. Season with salt, and add a good squeeze of lemon juice just before serving.

Substitute orange (or tangerine) juice for the lemon, add finely grated rind and you have a MALTAISE SAUCE. Whipped cream added to a *Hollandaise* makes a MOUSSELINE SAUCE, which is served cold.

Summer

The new season has arrived, bringing a glut of home-grown and imported produce. Markets overflow with an excess of peaches and nectarines, apricots and fat red Californian plums. Asparagus are at their peak until the last spears are cut on Midsummer's Day at the end of June.

For many people summer in England begins with strawberries and cream and the Wimbledon finals. Although imported strawberries are now available in January, there is a peculiar pleasure in enjoying them in their proper season. Gooseberries, raspberries, red currants, loganberries, blackberries and cherries are among the fruits that do not yet break the bound of seasons and their short lease should be enjoyed to the full. Some of these soft fruits form the ingredients of summer pudding – another seasonal treat. The market stalls are full of vegetables and of the many varieties of salad leaves that are now available beside the ubiquitous lettuce. French greengages and mirabelles, cultivated blueberries, watermelons, heavily scented charentais … the list is endless. Summer picnics and gooseberry fool or raspberry tart are among the true delights of an all too short season.

CREAM OF LETTUCE AND CUCUMBER SOUP

A quick and delicious blender soup.
Makes four servings.

	Imperial	Metric	American
Lettuce – 2			
Shallots – 3			
Butter	1 oz	30 g	2 tbsp
Cucumber – half			
Garlic clove – 1			
Fresh basil – 1 large sprig			
Salt and pepper			
Single (coffee) cream	2 tbsp	2 tbsp	3 tbsp

Peel and chop the shallots and sauté in butter until soft. Peel and slice the cucumber, toss the slices with the shallots. Shred the lettuce and add that, with the chopped garlic, a good sprig of fresh basil, salt and pepper to taste. Add 1 pint/600 ml/2½ cups of water, bring to the boil, and simmer for 5 minutes. Throw everything into the blender and switch on to produce a smooth soup. Add the cream, taste again for seasoning. Serve hot with croûtons.

PISTOU SOUP

A thick vegetable soup, flavoured with basil and garlic, made throughout the eastern Côte d'Azur and adjacent Italy. The variety and quantity of vegetables changes according to season and availability, but beans are a staple ingredient.
Makes eight servings.

	Imperial	Metric	American
Haricot beans	4 oz	115 g	¼ lb
Assorted vegetables: leeks, carrots, a turnip, a medium-sized onion, courgettes (zuchini), celery, potatoes, tomatoes, French beans – of each ingredient:	4–6 oz	115–170 g	4–6 oz
Bay leaf – 1			
Salt and black pepper			
Pasta	2 oz	55 g	2 oz
Tomato puree	2 tbsp	2 tbsp	3 tbsp
Garlic cloves – 1 or 2			
Basil – 1 large sprig			
Oil	2 tbsp	2 tbsp	3 tbsp
Parmesan cheese	1 tbsp	1 tbsp	1 tbsp

Soak the haricot beans overnight. Boil until tender–about 45 minutes–or use 1 × 5 oz (140 g) can.

Prepare the vegetables, peel the potatoes, skin and chop the tomatoes, turnip,

carrots, onion, celery and French beans. Put in a large stewpan with 2½ pints/
1·5 litres/1½ quarts of water, the bay leaf, salt and pepper. After 15 minutes'
simmering, add the beans, the pasta, and a good squeeze of tomato puree.
Simmer for a further 15 minutes.

Meanwhile, make a pistou by pounding a clove or two of garlic with a good
sprig of chopped basil (some cooks would add a handful). Add the oil and
parmesan cheese.

Stir the sauce into the soup just before serving. Serve with crusty French
bread, and pass around a bowl of freshly grated parmesan.

TOMATO MOUSSE

Makes four servings.

	Imperial	Metric	American
Large tomatoes – 6			
Butter	1 oz	30 g	2 tbsp
Onion – half			
Mushrooms	2 oz	55 g	½ cup
Cloves – 2			
Fresh tarragon – a few sprigs			
Sugar	1 tsp	1 tsp	1 tsp
Salt and pepper			
Gelatine as required			
Double (whipping) cream	5 oz	150 ml	⅔ cup

Plunge tomatoes into boiling water for 1 minute to loosen their skins. Skin them,
remove seeds and chop tomatoes finely. Sauté the chopped onion in a little
heated butter until soft, then add tomatoes, the finely-chopped mushrooms, the
cloves, tarragon, and the sugar. Simmer until tomatoes are cooked and soft,
remove the cloves, and pass through a fine sieve, or puree in an electric blender.
Taste for seasoning, adding salt and pepper as needed.

Whip the cream till stiff.

Dissolve gelatine in hot water, you will need enough to set a pint of puree,
according to the maker's instructions – as a rough guide it will be about
½ oz/15 g gelatine to 1 pint/600 ml/2½ cups of liquid. Stir gelatine into the puree
in a bowl, and leave to set.

As it begins to set, fold in the whipped cream, and pour into a suitable mould,
wetted with cold water. Refrigerate until firm.

Serve as a starter or as part of a cold buffet.

ONIONS A LA GRECQUE

'A la grecque' means cooked in a marinade and served cold. Many sorts of vegetables can be prepared in this way – mushrooms are perhaps the most popular in the repertoire, although onions, cauliflower, turnips, radishes, leeks and courgettes are equally good.

	Imperial	Metric	American
Pickling onions	8 oz	225 g	½ lb
Tomatoes	8 oz	225 g	½ lb
Coriander seeds	1 tsp	1 tsp	1 tsp
Cummin seeds	1 tsp	1 tsp	1 tsp
Fresh coriander – 1 sprig			
Fresh parsley – several sprigs			
White wine	4 fl oz	115 ml	½ cup
Olive oil	2 tbsp	2 tbsp	3 tbsp
Salt			
Whole black peppercorns	1 tsp	1 tsp	1 tsp
Tiny chilli peppers – optional			

Boil the onions for 5 minutes in their skins. Plunge tomatoes into boiling water for 1 minute to loosen their skins. Skin them, de-seed and chop finely. Skin the onions. Put onions, tomatoes and the rest of the ingredients in a pan, bring to the boil and simmer for 30 minutes, or until the onions are tender. Leave to get cold.

Vegetables *à la grecque* improve overnight, and are at their best within 24 hours.

AVOCADO DIP

Makes four servings.

	Imperial	Metric	American
French mustard	1 tsp	1 tsp	1 tsp
Egg yolks – 2			
Garlic clove – quarter			
Olive oil	4 fl oz	125 ml	½ cup
Small avocado pear – 1			
White wine vinegar			
or lemon juice	1 tsp	1 tsp	1 tsp

Put the mustard, the egg yolks and a speck of minced garlic in a mixing bowl. Beat the yolks and add the oil drop by drop until you have a thick mayonnaise.

Put the pulp of the avocado in a blender with the vinegar, and reduce to a puree, or press through a fine sieve. Blend with the mayonnaise to make a smooth green sauce – you can add a few drops of green colouring if you like. Add salt to taste and additional vinegar (or lemon juice) to thin the sauce to the desired consistency.

Use as a dip with bits of raw vegetables. This sauce is also very good on cold, sliced sweet potatoes, sprinkled with chopped chives.

BROCHETTES OF VEGETABLES WITH SATAY SAUCE

Makes four servings.

FOR THE BROCHETTES

	Imperial	Metric	American
Pickling onions – 8			
Green or red pimentos (sweet pepper) – 2			
Medium-sized mushrooms – not button mushrooms as they split on skewer – 8			
Tomatoes – 4			
Mint leaves – 1 bunch			
Aubergine (eggplant) – 1 or courgettes (zucchini) – 2			
Oil			

FOR THE MARINADE

	Imperial	Metric	American
Thin honey	1 tbsp	1 tbsp	1 tbsp
Small onion – 1			
Garlic – 1 clove			
Ginger	1 tsp	1 tsp	1 tsp
Ground coriander	1 tsp	1 tsp	1 tsp
Chilli powder	½ tsp	½ tsp	½ tsp
Salt			
Lemon	2 tbsp	2 tbsp	3 tbsp

FOR THE SAUCE

	Imperial	Metric	American
Unsalted peanuts	4 oz	115 g	¼ lb
Oil	1 tbsp	1 tbsp	1 tbsp
Thin honey	1 tbsp	1 tbsp	1 tbsp
Paprika	2 tsp	2 tsp	2 tsp
Chilli powder	½ tsp	½ tsp	½ tsp
Onion puree	1 tbsp	1 tbsp	1 tbsp
Tomato puree	2 tsp	2 tsp	2 tsp
Water	2 fl oz	55 ml	¼ cup

Boil the pickling onions until tender. Cut up the de-seeded peppers, onions and tomatoes but leave mushrooms whole. The vegetables should be cut into bite-size pieces to thread on the barbecue skewers. Mix marinade ingredients together, using the onion chopped very finely. Marinate vegetables for 2 hours or more, turning now and then.

Make the *satay* sauce by frying the peanuts in oil until golden, then pulverising them in a mortar or electric blender. Put into a saucepan with the onion juice, honey, spices, add a generous squeeze of tomato puree and the water. Bring to simmer, adding more water if the sauce becomes too thick – it should be of a creamy consistency.

Skewer pieces of vegetables alternatively with mint leaves, brush with oil and cook under a hot grill, or over a barbecue.

Serve the brochettes to dip in the *satay* sauce. This dish can be accompanied by the rice pilaff (page 51).

RATATOUILLE

A rich and aromatic vegetable stew, in which the principal ingredients are cooked separately, so that they retain their individual flavours, rather than one over-powering the rest during the cooking. Proportions and ingredients can vary, depending on what the cook has to hand. In Provence, where the recipe originated (if not in Italy . . .) the ingredients include tomatoes, courgettes, aubergines, green peppers, garlic – the sweet Provençal garlic – and the local, pungent herbs such as wild thyme, basil, bay and marjoram, stewed with olive oil. The result can be incomparable.

Makes six servings.

	Imperial	Metric	American
Tomatoes	1 lb	450 g	1 lb
Olive oil, approx.	5 fl oz	150 ml	⅔ cup
Onions	1 lb	450 g	1 lb
Aubergines (eggplant) – 2			
Courgettes (zucchini)	1 lb	450 g	1 lb
Green peppers	1 lb	450 g	1 lb
Garlic cloves – 5			
Thyme ⎫			
Parsley ⎪ 1 bouquet			
Basil ⎬			
Bay ⎭			
Salt and pepper			

Plunge tomatoes in boiling water to loosen their skins. Skin, de-seed and chop roughly. Heat in a casserole 1 tablespoon of oil, the crushed or minced cloves of garlic, and the herbs, then add the tomatoes.

Slice the aubergines (eggplant) and courgettes (zucchini) in rounds. De-seed peppers and cut into strips. Slice onions finely. Sauté all these vegetables in different pans, using the remaining oil. Cook them slowly with a sprinkling each of salt and pepper. See that they don't stick to the pan, adding oil as needed. Each vegetable should be cooked according to its character and consistency – the peppers may take longer than the courgettes (zucchini) and the aubergines (eggplant).

When they are all ready, combine with the tomatoes, reduced as a sauce, with the herbs removed. Adjust seasoning.

LENTIL AND RICE PILAFF

Makes four servings.

	Imperial	Metric	American
Green lentils	4 oz	115 g	½ cup
Basmati rice	8 oz	225 g	1 cup
Oil	1 tbsp	1 tbsp	1 tbsp
Spring onions (scallions), chopped – 3			
Parsley – several sprigs			
Mint – large sprig			
Salt			

Wash and pick over lentils, soak for 1 hour covered in water. Put in a pan with tightly-fitting lid, add 1 pint/600 ml/2½ cups of salted water, bring to the boil, then simmer for 20 minutes or until lentils are soft but not mushy.

Measure the reduced liquid, you should have approximately ¾ pint/425 ml/almost 2 cups (if not make up with water). Pour back into pan with the lentils, add the rice plus additional 2 fl oz/55 ml/¼ cup of water, and the sprig of mint. Cook, covered, on the lowest possible heat for 20 minutes, then leave with heat off for 5 minutes.

Stir with a fork, adding oil, chopped spring onions (scallions) and parsley. (See following recipe.)

RICE AND VEGETABLE PILAFF

Utilise any left-over pilaff or make up half the recipe on page 51. Use a paella *pan – a* paellera *– if you have one, or a wide frying pan. This dish allows considerable improvisation: you can use curry paste, a dash of tabasco, or harissa paste. Moisten with a glass of white wine, or sherry; add a squeeze of tomato puree, or a dash of Worcestershire sauce.*

Makes four servings.

	Imperial	Metric	American
Medium-sized onion – 1			
Vegetable oil	1 tbsp	1 tbsp	1 tbsp
Curry powder or garam masala	1 tbsp	1 tbsp	1 tbsp
Chilli powder	½ tsp	½ tsp	½ tsp
Courgettes (zucchini) or small sliced mushrooms	4 oz	115 g	¼ lb
Small cauliflower – 1			

Chop a medium-sized onion and sauté in hot oil until soft. Add curry powder to taste, or 1 tablespoon of garam masala and ½ teaspoon chilli powder.

Throw in sliced courgettes (zucchini), sliced mushrooms, cauliflower flowerets, strips of pepper, spring onions, or whatever vegetables you have to hand. Stir-fry together, with salt and black pepper, adding extra oil as needed. When vegetables are *al dente*, add the cooked rice pilaff, and stir together.

TOMATOES PROVENÇAL

These stuffed tomatoes are a familiar garnish to fish and meat dishes throughout the South of France, they utilise the basic regional flavourings of garlic, olive oil, herbs and, of course, tomatoes.

Makes four servings.

	Imperial	Metric	American
Tomatoes, depending on size – 4 or 8			
Small onion – 1			
Garlic cloves – 1 or 2			
Parsley – several sprigs			
Breadcrumbs	4 oz	115 g	1 cup
Olive oil	2 tbsp	2 tbsp	2 tbsp
Vegetable oil	4 tbsp	4 tbsp	5 tbsp

Preheat oven to 200° C/400° F/Gas Mark 6.

Choose big, meaty tomatoes if you can find them, the open-air, close-to-the-ground variety, rather than those nurtured in a greenhouse. Slice them across and scoop out the pulp and seeds into a bowl.

Finely chop the onion, mince the garlic, and stew together with the pulp in heated olive oil over a gentle heat until soft. Chop the parsley and mix with breadcrumbs. Fry the crumb/parsley mixture in 3 tablespoons of oil until golden, then mix with the tomato/onion mixture. Season with salt and pepper.

Fill hollows in each tomato with the mixture. Drizzle with oil and bake for 15–20 minutes or until top forms a golden crust, and tomatoes are soft. Serve hot or cold.

PEPPER SALAD

Some supermarkets sell red, yellow and green peppers in packs of three. If you buy them loose, choose more red than green ones, but aim for a variation in colours.
Makes four servings.

	Imperial	Metric	American
Pimentos (sweet peppers) – 3 or 4			
Tomatoes	8 oz	225 g	½ lb
Oil	¼ pint	150 ml	⅔ cup
Wine vinegar	2 tbsp	2 tbsp	3 tbsp
Paprika	1 tsp	1 tsp	1 tsp
Salt			
Black pepper			
Currants	1 tbsp	1 tbsp	1 tbsp

To each 1 lb/450 g of peppers use ½ lb/225 g tomatoes.

Grill the peppers under a hot grill, turning them as they burn and blister – this takes about 20 minutes. Wrap the peppers in a cloth for 5 minutes, after which they will be easy to skin. Remove the seeds and cut into narrow strips.

Plunge tomatoes in boiling water for 1 minute, to remove skins. De-seed and chop, add to peppers. Make a marinade of oil and vinegar and add paprika, salt, black pepper and currants. Pour over the peppers and leave for at least 3 hours, preferably overnight.

AVOCADO AND TOMATO ICE-CREAM

Some vegetables blend successfully with cream and mayonnaise to make a smooth and savoury ice-cream, which can be served as a starter. If you have an electric blender, avocado pears and tomatoes produce an ice with a delicate apricot colour and a refreshing flavour.
Makes four to six servings.

	Imperial	Metric	American
Ripe avocado pear – 1			
Tomatoes – 3 or 4			
Cucumber – 1			
Garlic clove – quarter			
Worcestershire sauce, optional	¼ tsp	¼ tsp	¼ tsp
Tomato puree	2 heaped tsp	2 heaped tsp	2 heaped tsp
Mayonnaise	4 heaped tbsp	4 heaped tbsp	5 heaped tbsp
Cream or soured cream	½ pint	275 ml	1⅓ cups
Salt and Cayenne pepper			

Plunge tomatoes in boiling water to loosen their skins. Skin and feed the flesh into the blender a little at a time with the flesh of the avocado, 1 half of the peeled cucumber and the garlic. Switch on full speed until smooth.

Add remaining ingredients and blend until smooth. Freeze mixture, turning over and stirring every hour to prevent ice crystals forming.

Shred the remaining cucumber. Allow 1 scoop of ice-cream for each person. Serve it in individual dishes, arranged on a bed of finely-shredded cucumber.

PEACH MELBA

Makes four servings.

	Imperial	Metric	American
Peaches or nectarines – 4			
Sugar	4 oz	115 g	½ cup
Fresh raspberries	8 oz	225 g	1⅔ cups
Vanilla ice-cream – 4 portions			
Vanilla flavouring-essence, vanilla pod or vanilla sugar			

Scald the peaches in boiling water to loosen their skins. Skin and cut in half to remove the stones. If the stones will not come out easily, poach fruit first and remove them later. Either way, put the skinned fruit in about ¾ pint/425 ml/ 2 cups water with 3 oz/85 g/generous ¼ cup of the sugar and the vanilla flavouring.

Cook until peaches are soft, drain, then leave to get cold.

Stew raspberries in remaining sugar until soft, and pass through a sieve to obtain a puree – there must be no tiny pips. Allow a generous portion of ice-cream for each serving, flanked by two peach halves and topped with the puree of raspberries.

PECHES DAME-BLANCHE

Prepare as above but omit the raspberry puree, and garnish instead with thin slices of pineapple, doused with kirsch. Decorate with whipped cream.

PECHES CARDINAL

Omit the ice-cream. Flavour the raspberry puree with kirsch. Decorate with toasted, flaked almonds.

PECHES AU COINTREAU

As the MELBA recipe, but douse peaches with Cointreau and use a strawberry puree in place of the raspberries.

ORANGE TART

To make 1 × 9″ (23 cm) tart (pie shell).

FOR THE PASTRY

	Imperial	Metric	American
Plain (all-purpose) flour	5 oz	140 g	1¼ cups
Chilled butter	3 oz	85 g	6 tbsp
Castor (fine granulated) sugar	2 oz	55 g	4 tbsp
Egg yolk – 1			
Iced water	1 tbsp	1 tbsp	1 tbsp

FOR THE FILLING

	Imperial	Metric	American
Medium-sized oranges – 12			
Sugar	6 oz	170 g	¾ cup
Eggs – 2			
Clear orange marmalade			

Rub the fat into the flour to the texture of breadcrumbs, add the sugar, then the yolk mixed with the water. Form into a dough, leave to rest. Roll it out to fit a 9″ (23 cm) tart or flan (pie shell) dish, line the dish. Set aside to rest in refrigerator for 20 minutes.

Preheat the oven to 180° C/350° F/Gas Mark 4.

Prick bottom of the flan, place in preheated oven and bake blind (with greaseproof (wax) paper lining and baking beans) for 15 minutes.

Whilst the pastry is chilling and then cooking, start making the filling. Boil 2 oranges in water for 20 minutes. Allow them to cool and put the orange and skin in an electric blender or liquidiser with the sugar, turn on full power to obtain a rich puree. Add the eggs, but only blend long enough to mix them in (too much blending will create a lot of air, which will expand during cooking, causing the filling to spill over the edge).

Remove the greaseproof (wax) paper and baking beans and pour in the orange puree. Bake the flan on the middle shelf at 150° C/300° F/Gas Mark 2 for 45 minutes.

Peel the remaining oranges, leaving some of the pith. Cut into thin slices – about ⅛″ (25 mm) – and boil in water for 10 minutes. Drain thoroughly. Arrange segments on the flan to overlap symmetrically, in a spiral, or two concentric circles, one within the other. Melt orange marmalade and glaze tart with a spoon and pastry brush. Leave to cool.

FRUIT FOOLS

In spite of the name, a fool is one of the most aristocratic of English dishes with an ancient lineage. According to the dictionary, the word 'fool' is synonymous with trifle, a thing of little account, but it probably derives from the French fouler – *to crush – and has Norman ancestry. The crushed or pulped fruit is blended with thick cream. The full flavour of the fruit is retained and sublimely amalgamated with the cream.*

Berry fruits are particularly suitable: raspberries, red currants, black currants, mulberries, gooseberries, but apricots, pears and apples also make good fools.

Makes four servings.

	Imperial	Metric	American
Black currants	1 lb	450 g	4 cups
Water	3 tbsp	3 tbsp	Scant ¼ cup
Castor (fine granulated) sugar	5 oz	150 g	⅔ cup
Double (whipping) cream	10 fl oz	300 ml	1¼ cups

Strip the black currants from their stalks with a fork, wash and drain to remove bits of leaf and stalk. Stew them in a pan with about 3 tablespoons of water until soft enough to pass through a sieve to remove skin and pips. You will be left with about ½ pint/300 ml/1¼ cups of puree.

Return a third of this puree to the pan with the sugar and stir over a moderate heat until dissolved. Add remaining puree and leave to get quite cold.

Whip cream until stiff and fold into the puree, then pour into individual glasses and chill for at least 3 hours – preferably overnight. Serve with sponge fingers or langues de chat.

You can also make a delicious fool with Bramley apples, stewed with sugar and a little water, and flavoured with lemon peel, whipped to a fine puree and mixed with thick cream.

LEMON TART

This recipe really does need a blender/liquidiser.
To make 1 × 8″ (20 cm) flan (pie shell).

FOR THE PASTRY

	Imperial	Metric	American
Plain (all purpose) flour	6 oz	170 g	1½ cups
Castor (fine granulated) sugar	1 tbsp	1 tbsp	1 tbsp
Salt – 1 pinch			
Butter	4 oz	115 g	½ cup
Egg yolk – 1			
Cold water	2 tsp	2 tsp	2 tsp

FOR THE FILLING

	Imperial	Metric	American
Lemons – 2			
Water	1 tbsp	1 tbsp	1 tbsp
Sugar	8 oz	225 g	1 cup
Eggs – 2			

Put the flour, sugar and salt in a mixing bowl. Cut up the butter in small pieces and rub into the flour until it resembles breadcrumbs. Add the egg yolk mixed in with the water, stir and form into a dough. Roll out the pastry, fit in the tart (pie shell) dish, and leave to rest for 1 hour.

Preheat oven to 200° C/400° F/Gas Mark 6.

Prick bottom of the pastry with a fork, and use toasted crusts and baking beans to hold pastry in place while it cooks. Bake blind for about 7 minutes.

Make the filling by simmering the lemons for 20 minutes. Put them in the blender/liquidiser goblet with 1 tablespoon of water, and switch on to full speed to pulverise the lemons. Then add the sugar, and switch on for a few seconds. Add the eggs, and blend for only 2 or 3 seconds – if you beat the eggs too long, they incorporate a lot of air, swell in the hot oven, and spill out over the side of the dish. If you balk at the idea of whole, pulverised lemons, skin, pips and all, which makes a really tangy, bittersweet tart, remove some of the peel, and the pips, before blending.

Lower oven temperature to 170° C/325° F/Gas Mark 3.

Pour the mixture into the tart (pie shell) case, and bake on the middle shelf for 35–40 minutes. If, during the baking, the mixture threatens to spill over, turn down the temperature. It will rise slightly, and turn golden brown on top. When cool, glaze the surface with a syrup made from 2 teaspoons of sugar and 1 tablespoon of water boiled for 2 or 3 minutes. Serve lukewarm, just as it is – cream or any other sauce doesn't really compliment this tart.

58

STRAWBERRY ICE PROFITEROLES

This is a confection of choux *paste balls, stuffed with strawberry ice-cream, topped with a strawberry sauce.*
Makes four to six servings.

FOR THE ICE-CREAM

	Imperial	Metric	American
Sugar	3 oz	85 g	6 tbsp
Water	2 tbsp	2 tbsp	3 tbsp
Strawberries	8 oz	225 g	1⅔ cups
Double (whipping) cream	5 oz	140 g	⅔ cup

FOR THE CHOUX PASTRY

Butter	3 oz	85 g	⅓ cup
Plain (all purpose) flour	4 oz	115 g	1 cup
Large eggs – 2			
Water	½ pint	275 ml	1¼ cups
Salt – 1 pinch			

FOR THE SAUCE

Red currant jelly	4 oz	115 g	⅓ cup
Strawberries	8 oz	225 g	1⅔ cups
Cornflour (cornstarch)	3 oz	85 g	⅔ cup
Orange juice	3 tbsp	3 tbsp	Scant ¼ cup
Whole strawberries for decoration			

TO MAKE THE ICE-CREAM

Dissolve the sugar in the water in a small pan. Boil for exactly 1 minute. Make a puree of the strawberries in a blender or through a sieve. Add the syrup to the puree. Whip the cream until stiff, fold into the puree until there are no streaks, and put in the freezer, stirring at intervals to prevent ice crystals from forming.

TO MAKE THE PASTRY

Preheat oven to 210° C/410° F/Gas Mark 6–7.

Melt the butter in the water in a suitable pan. Bring to the boil, then remove from the heat and add the sieved flour and salt all at once. Beat until the paste leaves the sides of the pan. Leave to cool, then beat in 2 eggs to make a smooth paste. Use a piping bag, or a teaspoon, to make little mounds, roughly the size of a chestnut, on a greased baking sheet. Bake for 20 minutes on the middle shelf. Remove from the oven and make a slit in the side of each ball to allow the steam to escape. Leave to cool on a wire rack.

TO MAKE THE SAUCE

Melt the jelly in orange juice over a moderate heat. Add cornflour (cornstarch) mixed to a smooth paste with a little cold water. Boil for 2–3 minutes to thicken, then take off the heat. Allow to cool a little before adding the pureed straw-berries.

Stuff each profiterole with ice-cream, pile on a serving dish, coat with the sauce, and decorate with whole strawberries.

PEACHES A LA DIABLE

Peaches or nectarine dessert, served with macaroons.
Makes four servings.

	Imperial	Metric	American
Peaches or nectarines – 1 per head			
Sugar	1 tbsp	1 tbsp	1 tbsp
Vanilla essence or vanilla sugar			
Ground almonds	4 oz	115 g	1 cup
Rice flour	1 oz	30 g	1 oz
Castor (fine granulated) sugar	6 oz	170 g	¾ cup
Egg whites – 2			
Kirsch liqueur – 1 sprinkle/peach			
Peach preserve	1 tsp	1 tsp	1 tsp
Icing (confectioner's) sugar			
Whipped cream			

Plunge the peaches into boiling water to loosen skins. Skin peaches, cut in half to remove the stone. If the stones are stubborn, remove them after poaching. Put the peaches in a pan covered with water, adding 1 tablespoon of sugar for each peach and the vanilla flavouring. Simmer until fruit is soft (depending on ripeness). Drain.

Preheat the oven to 190° C/375° F/Gas Mark 5.

To make a batch of macaroons: beat egg whites until stiff, fold in the almonds, rice flour and sugar to make a stiffish paste. Grease a baking sheet and liberally dust with rice flour. Put small heaps of the mixture, about a teaspoon at a time, on the baking sheet, about 2–3″ (5–7.5 cm) apart. Bake for 10–15 minutes until light brown. Quickly lift from sheet with a spatula to prevent them sticking.

When you are ready to serve, allow two macaroons per person, and sprinkle with a little kirsch. Nap with a spoonful of peach preserve, top each macaroon with a halved peach, and dust with icing sugar. Put in a hot oven for 5 minutes, and serve with whipped cream.

PAVLOVA CAKE

This Australian delicacy of meringue with fruit and cream, contains by tradition the pulp of passion fruits with whole strawberries, but you can use raspberries alone, or with other suitable berry fruits. Legend says that the cake was invented by a Melbourne chef in honour of Anna Pavlova, who was touring Australia, accompanied by a retinue of dancers and a hundred songbirds in golden cages.

To make 1 × 9″ (23 cm) cake.

	Imperial	Metric	American
Egg whites – 3			
Salt – 1 pinch			
Castor (fine granulated) sugar	3 oz	85 g	6 tbsp
Vinegar, malt or white wine	1 tsp	1 tsp	1 tsp
Cornflour (cornstarch)	1 tsp	1 tsp	1 tsp
Vanilla essence – a few drops			
Cream of tartar	½ tsp	½ tsp	½ tsp
Double (whipping) cream	5 oz	140 g	⅔ cup
Strawberries	1 lb	450 g	2 cups
Passion fruits – 3			

Preheat oven to 140° C/275° F/Gas Mark 1–2.

Beat the egg whites until stiff with the salt, then beat in one third of the sugar with the vanilla and vinegar. Mix the cornflour (cornstarch) and cream of tartar with the remaining sugar, and fold into the meringue.

Cut a 9″ (23 cm) disc of greaseproof (wax) paper, oil it well. Place over a baking sheet, and spoon the meringue to form a circle, the base wider than the top (the original design was probably meant to represent the ballet dancer's tutu).

Bake in a cool oven for about 45 minutes to 1 hour. The meringue should be white, or the very palest brown, crisp on the outside but soft inside.

When cold, carefully remove the paper base, put the meringue on a serving dish, whip the cream and fill the centre, top with the hulled strawberries mixed with passion fruit pulp.

SUMMER PUDDING

Once known as Malvern pudding, this familiar dessert of summer fruits in a bread-lined bowl needs a little extra care to make. If the bread fails to become totally impregnated with the fruit juice, the finished pudding has a somewhat mottled, piebald appearance. Use staleish bread if possible, and preferably not from a pre-sliced sandwich loaf.

The pudding basin or bowl capacity depends on the quantity of fruit. You will need a 1½ pint/850 ml/3¾ cup capacity basin for 1½ lbs (680 g) of fruit; 3 pint/ 1.7 litre/7½ cup capacity for 3 lbs (1.4 kg). 3 lbs (1.4 kg) fruit will need 10 oz (290 g/1¼ cups) sugar.

Makes four servings.

	Imperial	Metric	American
Assorted fresh fruit – red currants, black currants, raspberries, but not strawberries	1½ lbs	680 g	1½ lbs
Granulated sugar	5–6 oz	140–170 g	⅝–¾ cup
Bread – 6 or 8 slices			
Whipped cream to serve			

Prepare the fruit, wash it and put it in a stewing pan with the sugar. Add 1 tablespoon or so of water and simmer until the fruit is soft. Drain the fruit syrup into a bowl. Tailor the bread to fit the basin: the bread should be cut in ½″ (1 cm) thick slices and the crusts trimmed off. Cut a disc to fit the bottom, and wide fingers of bread, overlapping for the sides. Dip each piece in the fruit syrup before assembling.

Fill with the fruit, and cut pieces of bread for the top. Put a saucer or plate on top, that fits in the basin, and weight it down. Refrigerate for several hours or overnight. To unmould the pudding, run a thin-bladed knife around it, invert on a serving dish. Serve with whipped cream.

SWEET POTATO TART

For preference choose the orange-fleshed sweet potato to give this tart a caramel colour and richness. It is flavoured with rum and almonds. First, make a pastry case (pie shell) as for the pear and almond tart, page 90.

To make 1 × 9″ (23 cm) tart (pie shell).

	Imperial	Metric	American
Sweet potatoes	1 lb	450–500 g	1 lb
Egg – 1			
Butter	1 oz	30 g	2 tbsp
Plain (all purpose) flour	3 oz	85 g	¾ cup
Castor (fine granulated) sugar	2 heaped tbsp	2 heaped tbsp	3 heaped tbsp
Vanilla essence or sugar			
Rum	1–2 tbsp	1–2 tbsp	2–3 tbsp
Cream to serve			

Preheat oven to 180° C/350° F/Gas Mark 4.

Bake the potatoes, peel away the skin, and puree the pulp. When cool add the egg, beaten, and the melted butter. Sift in the flour gradually. Add the almonds, sugar, and a few drops of vanilla essence, or vanilla sugar. Beat thoroughly with the rum. Pour into the prepared pastry case (pie shell) and bake for 40 minutes.

Glaze with a sugar syrup made with 1 oz/30 g/2 tbsp of sugar and 1 fl oz/30 ml/2 tbsp of water boiled for 1 minute. Serve warm with cream.

APRICOT AND GUAVA ICE-CREAM

An unusual combination of flavours, although this is a rather exaggerated claim when you consider the range of flavours and combinations offered by Howard Johnson's and Dayville's.
Makes four to six servings.

	Imperial	Metric	American
Fresh apricots	1 lb	450 g	1 lb
Guavas, fresh or tinned – 2			
Castor (fine granulated) sugar	1 tbsp	1 tbsp	1 tbsp
White wine	5 fl oz	150 ml	⅔ cup
Double (whipping) cream	5 fl oz	150 ml	⅔ cup

Preheat oven to 180° C/350° F/Gas Mark 4.

Halve and stone the apricots. Put in a heatproof ovenware dish with a lid, add the pulp of the guavas, the sugar and the wine. Bake for 45 minutes until soft, watch that the syrup formed by the fruit doesn't bubble over the dish into the oven. Leave to get cold.

Pass through a sieve, or puree in a blender. Whip the cream stiff and fold into the puree. Pour into a suitable container and freeze in the ice-making compartment of your refrigerator, stirring from time to time to prevent ice-crystals from forming.

FRUIT BRULE

A fruit salad with a topping of cream and caramel. You can vary the contents of the salad according to fruits in season.
Makes four to six servings.

FOR THE FRUIT SALAD

	Imperial	Metric	American
Dessert apples, sliced, chopped but unpeeled – 2			
Banana, chopped – 1			
Small melon to make melon balls – 1			
Kiwi fruit, peeled and sliced – 2			
Black grapes – 12			
Tin of mandarin oranges – 1			

FOR THE TOPPING

	Imperial	Metric	American
Castor (fine granulated) sugar	1 heaped tbsp	1 heaped tbsp	1 heaped tbsp
Double (whipping) cream	10 fl oz	300 ml	1¼ cups

Prepare the salad. Whip the cream until it sets, but is not too stiff. Put the salad in a serving dish and cover with the cream. Chill for 2 hours. Melt the sugar in a small pan over the heat, and after a minute or two it will start to caramelise. When all the sugar is dissolved, and brown, scatter it quickly over the cream and return to the refrigerator. Chill for a further hour before serving.

MAYONNAISE

As familiar as Béchamel *and, like* Béchamel, *the basis for several other sauces.*
To make approximately 7 fl oz/200 ml/1 scant cup.

	Imperial	Metric	American
Dijon mustard	1 tbsp	1 tbsp	1 tbsp
Egg yolk – 1			
Salt and pepper			
Oil	5 fl oz	150 ml	⅔ cup
Wine vinegar or lemon juice, optional	1–2 tsp	1–2 tsp	1–2 tsp

Put the Dijon mustard in a bowl, with an egg yolk and seasoning (these are the emulsifying agents). It is much easier to make this in a mixer bowl, but however you do it the process remains the same: add the oil, drop by drop until the sauce begins to take, and emulsify. You can then add the oil a little more quickly.

Should it separate, scrape into a bowl, crack another egg yolk in the mixing bowl, and add the failed mayonnaise drop by drop. If you want to thin the mayonnaise, add a little wine vinegar or lemon juice.

Some emulsified sauces are based on hard-boiled (cooked) egg yolks, mashed to a paste with a little mustard, then the oil is added as for mayonnaise. Such is the SAUCE TARTARE, with the addition of chopped chives, gherkins and capers.

A mayonnaise flavoured with curry powder becomes a SAUCE INDIENNE. For a NIÇOISE SAUCE, add finely-chopped green olives, pimento (sweet pepper) and a squeeze of tomato puree to a basic mayonnaise.

The popular SAUCE VERTE is a puree of herbs, or very finely-chopped herbs, such as tarragon, chives, parsley and chervil added to the sauce in sufficient quantity to colour it a delicate green.

AÏOLI

This thick, garlic-flavoured mayonnaise of Provence is usually eaten with boiled vegetables and fish; it is also a good accompaniment to plainly boiled sweet potatoes, and as a dip for a variety of crudités. The term aïoli usually refers to the prepared dish of cod, boiled potatoes, carrots, beans etc, served with the sauce.

To make approximately 5 fl oz/150 ml/⅔ cup.

	Imperial	Metric	American
Egg yolks – 2			
Garlic cloves – 4 or 5			
Salt – 1 pinch			
Olive oil, approx.	2 fl oz	55 ml	¼ cup
Lemon juice } optional	1 tbsp	1 tbsp	1 tbsp
Water	1 tsp	1 tsp	1 tsp

Put the egg yolks in a bowl with 4 or 5 crushed cloves of garlic and a little salt. Add, drop by drop, stirring continuously, sufficient olive oil to make a thick mayonnaise. The sauce can be thinned down with lemon juice and a little water if needed.

A similar strongly flavoured sauce, made piquant by the addition of chillis, is the ROUILLE, which is from Marseilles and the surrounding area. Some versions are simply breadcrumbs, pounded with garlic and chilli peppers, thinned with olive oil. The more familiar ROUILLE, served with Bouillabaisse and fish soup is a MAYONNAISE or AÏOLI with the addition of a spoonful of Moroccan *harissa* (a red pepper sauce). Alternatively you can substitute chilli powder, or crushed dried chillis.

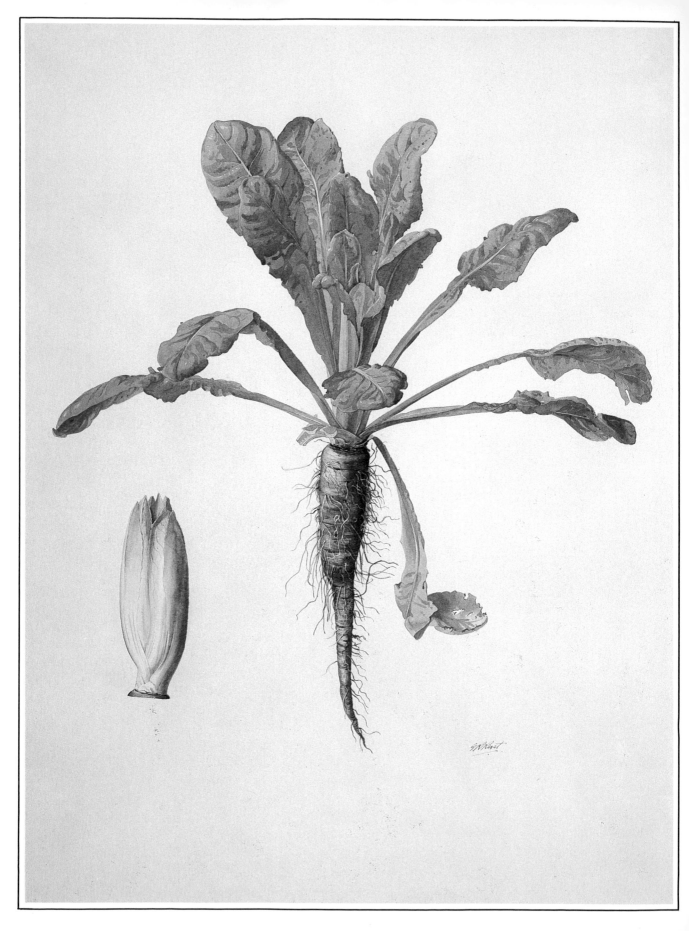

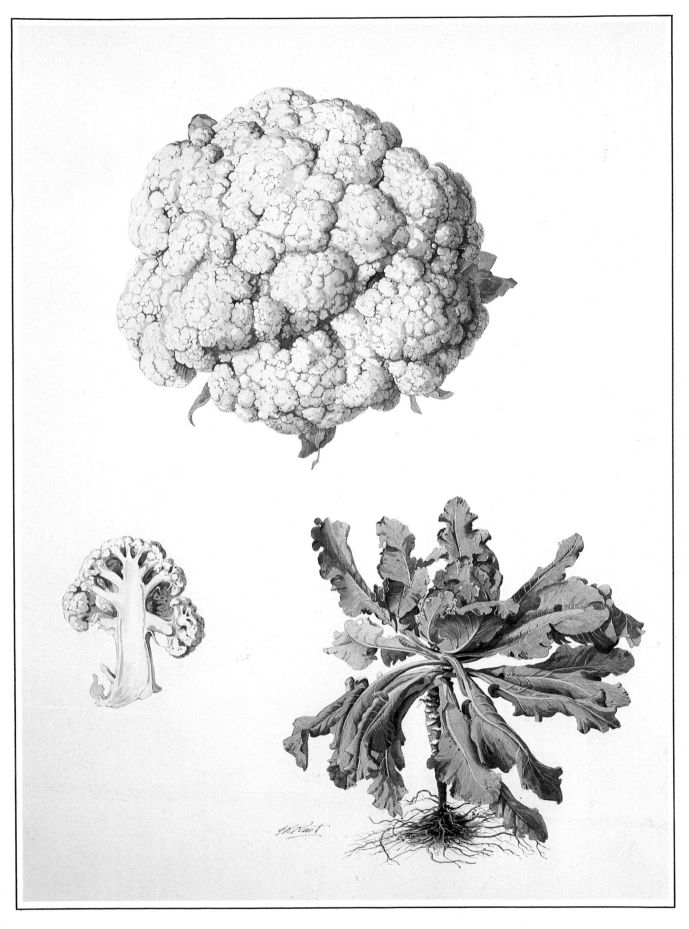

Autumn

The abundance of summer continues well into the autumn and in the markets, the barrows are stacked high with the seasons's fresh home-grown sweetcorn. The pick-your-own fruit farms are about to close their doors for the year but it is time to rove the hedgerows to pick wild blackberries to accompany the first Bramley apples in a blackberry and apple pie, one of the glories of autumn cooking.

On the markets look out for the probable glut of apples and pears, but also for courgettes and globe artichokes. Among imported fruits, fresh figs, persimmons and pomegranates should not be missed.

In France, autumn is the much-awaited season of the wild *fungi*, ceps in particular. The first ceps fetch high prices on the markets of Bordeaux. The growing band of British cep-fanciers keep a sharp eye on the specialist greengrocers. Where to find wild ceps in the woods or the apricot-coloured chanterelle, is a closely-guarded secret among the aficionados.

Autumn is also the season for pickle- and chutney-making. As the first frost nips the sloes in the hedgerows, it is time to harvest them and prepare a supply of body-warming sloe-gin, in time for Christmas.

On the Continent, autumn is synonymous with the wine harvest and in the Medoc region of France, for instance, the grapes will be watched by the hour to pick the exact moment for the *vendange*, particularly when the weather is unpredictable. In Alsace and in the Rhineland, the colder climate makes it imperative to keep the grapes on the vines as long as possible and the Riesling harvest often does not start before early November.

BORSCHT

It isn't easy to make small quantities of borscht – essentially it is a filling soup with strips of vegetables, coloured a rich pinkish-red by the beetroot, and a mere 1 lb (450 g) of beetroot goes a long way.

Makes six to eight servings.

	Imperial	Metric	American
Raw beetroot	1 lb	450 g	1 lb
Carrots – 2 or 3			
Medium-sized parsnip – 1			
Large onion – 1			
Celery sticks (stalks) – 3 or 4			
Water	1¾ pints	1 litre	1 quart
Tomatoes	1 × 8 oz tin	1 × 225 g tin	1 × ½ lb can
Sugar	2 tsp	2 tsp	2 tsp
Bay leaves – 2			
Salt and pepper to taste			
Cabbage heart – 1			
Butter	1 oz	30 g	2 tbsp
Vinegar	1 tbsp	1 tbsp	1 tbsp
Cream and chopped dill for decoration			

Peel, slice and cut beetroot into matchstick strips, likewise the carrots, parsnip, onion and celery. Put vegetables in a large pan and cover with water. Chop and add the tomatoes, the sugar, the bay leaves, salt and pepper (1 teaspoon of salt, then taste for more at the end of cooking time). Simmer for 15 minutes, then add the butter, the finely-shredded cabbage, and the vinegar.

Let the soup simmer for 1 hour. If you have a liquidiser/blender you can thicken the soup by taking two good ladlefuls of soup and vegetables and reducing that to a puree – add to the soup. Serve with a dash of cream and a sprinkling of dill.

SWEET 'N' HOT CORN AND OKRA CHOWDER

This is a cross between a chowder and a gumbo soup. The corn provides the sweetness. Chillis add a fiery piquancy, while the okra – also known as ladies' fingers – gives the dish a delicate, mucilaginous texture.

Makes four servings.

	Imperial	Metric	American
Fresh corns on-the-cob – 2			
Onion, medium-sized – 1			
Celery stalks (sticks) – 2			
Oil for frying			
Okra	8 oz	225 g	½ lb
Milk/water mixed half and half	1 pint	600 ml	2½ cups
Dry chillis – 2			
Salt and pepper			

Boil the ears of corn for 5 minutes, leave to cool, or plunge into cold water. Sauté finely-chopped onion and finely-sliced celery in oil. Slice and add okra, stir-fry for a minute or two until the vegetables begin to soften. Strip corn from the husk and add to the onion/okra mixture.

Put these fried vegetables in a stewpan, add the milk/water mixture, the chillis, the salt and pepper. Simmer for 30 minutes on a low flame.

To make a smoother soup, you can blend a third of the volume, then add to the rest. The soup improves by keeping overnight and reheating the following day. Remove chillis before serving.

CHEESE AND ONION ROULADE

Makes six servings.

	Imperial	Metric	American
Puff pastry	12 oz	340 g	¾ lb
Feta cheese, or ricotta	8 oz	225 g	½ lb
Grated cheddar cheese	2 oz	55 g	½ cup
Spring onions (scallions) – 6			
Parsley – several sprigs			
Chives – a few			
Black pepper			
Eggs – 2			
Poppy seeds – optional	¼ tsp	¼ tsp	¼ tsp

Preheat oven to 200° C/400° F/Gas Mark 6.

Roll out pastry to a rectangle 15″ × 12″ (37 cm × 30 cm). Leave to rest. Meanwhile, crumble the feta, mix with grated cheddar, finely-sliced spring onions, a few chopped chives, a generous handful of finely-chopped parsley and some black pepper. Add beaten eggs and blend thoroughly.

Pile mixture onto centre of pastry, then spread evenly to within 1½″ (4 cm) from the edge. Roll up like a Swiss roll, fairly loosely. Moisten edges with a wet pastry brush, seal along the long edge, then the ends, turning under to form a neat parcel or sausage shape with the long seam underneath. Brush with egg yolk and sprinkle with a few poppy seeds.

Bake for 30 minutes or until nicely browned. Can be served hot or cold with a green salad.

MUSHROOMS ON TOAST

Makes four servings.

	Imperial	Metric	American
Slices of white bread from a sandwich loaf – 2			
Mushrooms	4 oz	115 g	1 cup
Butter	3 oz	85 g	6 tbsp
Oil	4 tbsp	4 tbsp	5 tbsp
Cream	2 tbsp	2 tbsp	3 tbsp
Salt and pepper			
Parsley – a few sprigs			

Trim bread of its crusts. Fry lightly in half the heated butter, sufficiently to impregnate bread on both sides. Set aside on a plate. If you use button mushrooms, leave whole, otherwise slice in half. Sauté mushrooms over gentle heat in the remaining butter and half the oil. Season with salt and pepper.

Pour oil in a clean frying pan and bring to a high heat. Fry the bread slices until golden brown. This seals the bread and prevents it from going soggy when covered with mushrooms in their cream sauce.

Finely chop parsley. Drain mushrooms of juices and oil, stir in cream, warm over the flame for a moment, then pour over the fried bread slices. Sprinkle with parsley.

Morels can be prepared in a similar way for MORILLES A LA CREME:

	Imperial	Metric	American
Morels	4 oz	115 g	1 cup
Butter	3 oz	85 g	6 tbsp
Salt and pepper			
Nutmeg – 1 pinch			
White wine	4 fl oz	115 ml	½ cup
Cream	3–4 tbsp	3–4 tbsp	5–6 tbsp

Clean the morels, slice them, and boil for 10 minutes in a little water. Drain, then sauté in butter. Add salt, pepper and a grating of nutmeg. Cook in a covered pan, over a gentle heat, for about 1 hour, moistening from time to time with a little white wine.

Drain, then add fresh cream, and pour over the bread croûtes.

TERRINE OF AUBERGINE AND SWEET POTATO

Makes four to six servings.

	Imperial	Metric	American
Large aubergine (eggplant) – 1	12 oz	340 g	¾ lb
Sweet potatoes	12 oz	340 g	¾ lb
Fresh brown breadcrumbs	2 oz	50 g	1 cup
Oil	2–3 tbsp	2–3 tbsp	3–4 tbsp
Garlic clove – 1			
Chopped parsley	1 tbsp	1 tbsp	1 tbsp
Salt and pepper			

Peel the aubergine (eggplant), slice crosswise, and leave to sweat for about 30 minutes, then wash and pat dry. Meanwhile, boil the potatoes in their skins until just tender. Mince clove of garlic and mix in with breadcrumbs and chopped parsley.

Sauté aubergine (eggplant) slices in heated oil until they begin to soften and brown, then chop coarsely. Peel and chop the potatoes, mix with the aubergine (eggplant) and blend with two-thirds of the breadcrumb mixture. Season with salt and black pepper, bind with the beaten egg.

Preheat oven to 160° C/325° F/Gas Mark 3.

Press mixture into a suitable terrine mould, preferably oblong, or use a small loaf tin (pan). Quickly sauté the remaining breadcrumb mixture in the butter for 2 minutes, then spread evenly over the top of the aubergine (eggplant) mixture. Cover and bake for 1 hour.

Serve the terrine, cold, in slices with cold tomato *coulis* (see page 23) or one of the mayonnaise-based sauces (pages 67–68).

BROUILLADE DE TRUFFES

This dish combines fresh black truffles with scrambled eggs. It is apparently simple but needs careful timing. In place of fresh truffles you can successfully use tinned ones, or the white Italian truffles that sometimes appear on the market in season. In France, fresh truffles are wrapped with the eggs in their shells (the flavour permeates the albumen through the shell).

Makes four servings.

Truffle – 1
Eggs – 8 or 10
Salt

Chop the truffle as finely as possible.

In a pan, coddle the eggs. gently. They should be only just cooked, soft and not finely scrambled. It is better to turn them with a wooden spoon rather than a fork. Blend in the truffle as the eggs begin to set and add salt to taste. Serve with croûtons of bread fried in butter.

IMAM-BAYILDI

One of the best of the aubergine (eggplant) dishes. 'Imam Bayildi' is Turkish, and means 'The Priest Fainted' – probably from over-eating these stuffed delicacies. It is variously interpreted, but the old recipes say that Imam Bayildi *can be made with aubergines (eggplant) or courgettes (zucchini). A Turkish cookery book of the 1860s gives a recipe for aubergines stewed in water with onions and garlic. No mention in those days of tomatoes, olives and pine kernels, or curry powder or currants – all found in today's versions. In fact, these ingredients vastly improve the old recipe, as does a good sprinkling of parsley.*

Choose big, glossy aubergines. As a starter, a half aubergine per person should do, with four you will have two portions remaining – for the following day, or for hungry guests.

Makes six servings.

	Imperial	Metric	American
Aubergines (eggplant) – 4			
Medium-sized onions – 4			
Garlic cloves – 4			
Oil (approx.)	¼ pint	150 ml	½ cup
Curry paste or powder	1 tsp	1 tsp	1 tsp
Sugar	1 tsp	1 tsp	1 tsp
Salt and pepper			
Tomatoes, fresh	1 lb	450 g	1 lb
or canned	1 (14 oz)	1 (400 g)	1 (14 oz)
Chopped parsley			

Slice aubergines (eggplant) lengthwise in half. Scoop out the pulp and seeds to form boat-shaped shells. Plunge these into boiling water for 5 minutes, then refresh with cold water. If the aubergines are over-ripe, they may require less blanching; the shells should be thick and firm enough to hold their shape when stuffed.

Preheat oven to 180° C/350° F/Gas Mark 4.

Chop the pulp, finely chop the onions and garlic. Heat the oil and stir-fry the onions with the curry paste or curry powder until soft. Add the aubergine (eggplant) pulp, garlic, sugar, salt and pepper. You will probably need a good quantity of oil, as aubergines soak it up.

Add the tomatoes, skinned and chopped. Include the juice if they are canned. Stir and simmer until the consistency is thick.

Fill each shell with the mixture, put them in an ovenproof dish, with 1 tablespoonful of oil on the bottom, and bake for 30–45 minutes, or until the aubergines are soft. Baste occasionally during cooking. Serve lukewarm, or cold, sprinkled with parsley.

STUFFED CABBAGE A LA TURQUE

'Turkish' on account of its slightly exotic stuffing: pine nuts, currants, capers and some spicy sauces are among the ingredients. First make sure you have a casserole with a lid, deep enough to take a whole cabbage. Look for a really nice Savoy or winter cabbage.

Makes six servings.

	Imperial	Metric	American
Long grain rice	1½ tbsp	1½ tbsp	2 tbsp
Large aubergine (eggplant) – 1			
Large onion – 1			
Oil	1 tbsp	1 tbsp	1 tbsp
Cloves of garlic – 1 or 2			
Savoy or winter cabbage – 1			
Mushrooms	8 oz	225 g	2–2½ cups
Can of tomatoes	1 × 14 oz	1 × 400 g	1 × 14 oz
Pine kernels or flaked almonds	2 tsp	2 tsp	2 tsp
Mixed herbs	¼ tsp	¼ tsp	¼ tsp
Currants	2 tsp	2 tsp	2 tsp
Chopped olives – a few			
Capers	1 tsp	1 tsp	1 tsp
Worcestershire sauce	1 tsp	1 tsp	1 tsp
Chilli or Tabasco sauce – a dash			
Salt and pepper			

TO MAKE THE FILLING

Boil rice in salted water, drain well when cooked. Cook aubergine (eggplant) for 15 minutes in boiling water, drain and plunge into cold water. Finely chop and sauté onion in a little heated oil with the minced garlic.

Wash the cabbage, remove any wilted leaves and plunge into a large pan of boiling water for 4 minutes, then plunge into cold water. Drain thoroughly, then cut a cavity in the centre about 2½″ (6 cm) across to take some of the stuffing. Slice this scooped-out heart finely and add to the sautéd onion.

Add chopped mushrooms and skinned, chopped aubergine (eggplant), cooking the mixed vegetables until soft. Drain the can of tomatoes (drink the juice), chop and add them to the rice and other ingredients in a bowl. Taste for seasoning.

TO STUFF THE CABBAGE

Preheat oven to 150° C/300° F/Gas Mark 2.

Fill the centre and spread the rest of the stuffing between the leaves, working outwards until the mixture is used up. Tie up with thread and place in your casserole with ½ pint/300 ml/1¼ cups of water. Cover and bake for at least 2½ hours. Check occasionally to see that it hasn't dried up, add more water if necessary but only enough to keep it moist. Serve from the casserole, or turn out carefully onto a warm serving dish.

CAPONATA

A sweet-sour vegetable dish from Sicily, and a member of the ratatouille family.
An excellent, versatile starter that can be eaten hot or cold.
   Makes four servings.

	Imperial	Metric	American
Aubergines (eggplant)	12–16 oz	340–450 g	¾–1 lb
Oil	2½–4 fl oz	70–115 ml	⅓–½ cup
Medium-sized onion – 1			
Tin of tomatoes	1 × 14 oz	1 × 400 g	1 × 14 oz
Celery stick (stalk) – half			
White wine vinegar	3 tbsp	3 tbsp	Scant ¼ cup
Sugar	1 heaped tbsp	1 heaped tbsp	1 heaped tbsp
Salt and pepper			
Pine kernels	2 tsp	2 tsp	2 tsp
Capers	1 tsp	1 tsp	1 tsp
Green olives, pitted – 12			
Pickled peppercorns (poivre vert), optional	1 tsp	1 tsp	1 tsp

Slice the aubergines (eggplant), then dice into ½" (1 cm) cubes. Fry until brown in the heated oil; they soak up quite a bit of oil, so the quantity you may need varies.

   Slice and dice the onion, and stir-fry until soft and golden. Put onion in a stewpan, add the tomatoes, chopped, and the sliced celery and aubergine (eggplant). Add vinegar, sugar, salt and pepper. Cook until the mixture is thick and well amalgamated – about 20 minutes, but watch out for burning. Stir in the pine kernels, capers and olives, roughly-chopped, and the peppercorns if desired. Serve with crusty French bread.

MICHON DAUPHINOIS

This is a robust, 'peasant' version of the gratin dauphinois, *where the sliced potatoes are cooked in a batter.*

Makes four to six servings.

	Imperial	Metric	American
Potatoes	12 oz	340 g	¾ lb
Plain (all purpose) flour	4 oz	115 g	1 cup
Egg – 1			
Milk	10 fl oz	275 ml	1¼ cups
Garlic clove – 1			
Butter	½ oz	15 g	1 tbsp
Salt and pepper			
Nutmeg	¼ tsp	¼ tsp	¼ tsp

Preheat oven to 180° C/350° F/Gas Mark 4.

Peel and slice potatoes ⅛″ (25 mm) thick. Whisk the flour, egg and milk to a batter. Take an oven-proof pyrex dish, rub it with a cut clove of garlic and smear with a little butter. Flavour with salt and pepper. Arrange the potatoes in the dish and pour batter over them. Dust with grated nutmeg and bake for 50 minutes to 1 hour, or until browned on top.

Serve with a main course.

BROWN VEGETABLE STEW

A thick, rich brown vegetable stew, sustaining and full of flavour.
   Makes four to six servings.

	Imperial	Metric	American
Brown lentils	4 oz	115 g	½ cup
Potatoes	1 lb	450 g	1 lb
Red onions			
Oil	4 fl oz	125 ml	½ cup
Celery stalks (sticks) – 2			
Carrots, medium-sized – 3	6 oz	170 g	6 oz
Mushrooms	8 oz	225 g	½ lb
Tomatoes – small can	8 oz	225 g	½ lb
Red kidney beans – large can	15 oz	425 g	15 oz
Red wine	4 fl oz	115 ml	½ cup
Water, approx.	1 pint	570 ml	2½ cups
Garlic clove – 1			
Oregano	1 tsp	1 tsp	1 tsp
Bay leaves – 2			
Worcestershire sauce	1 tsp	1 tsp	1 tsp

Soak the lentils for 1 hour. Peel and cut potatoes into large cubes. Peel and roughly chop onions.

   Sauté potatoes and onions in oil until they begin to brown. Add the sliced celery, cook for 2 minutes. Remove vegetables to a large stewpan.

   Scrape and chop carrots, lightly brown them in remaining oil, chop and add mushrooms. Add to the stewpan with the tomatoes, beans, lentils, wine, water, minced garlic, herbs, seasonings, and the Worcestershire sauce. Simmer for 1 hour, or until the vegetables are tender. Season to taste.

PARSNIP FRITTERS

Practically any vegetable responds well to being coated in batter and deep-fried. Whether you need to parboil them first, or to leave them raw depends on the cooking time of the vegetable. Slices of custard marrow (patty pan squash) merely require slicing raw and then dipping in the batter. The same applies to mushrooms and pieces of aubergine (eggplant). Artichoke bottoms are best pre-cooked and left to cool before dipping. Salsify, scorzonera, sweet potato, celeriac and parsnip need to be cooked through. Don't overcook them, though, in case they lose their shape – firm to the bite, or al dente is the best guide. Dip each piece of vegetable in flour before dipping in the batter.

Makes four to six servings.

	Imperial	Metric	American
Medium-sized parsnips – 3			
Plain (all purpose) flour	3 tbsp	3 tbsp	3 tbsp
Salt			
Oil	1 tbsp	1 tbsp	1 tbsp
Egg white – 1			
Bicarbonate of soda – 1 pinch			

Scrape the parsnips, cut them in pieces 1″–1½″ (2.5–4 cm). Boil in salted water until tender, then drain and leave to cool. Make the batter by mixing the flour with a little salt, adding the oil and enough warm water to make a creamy coating batter. Beat the egg white stiff, add a pinch of bicarbonate to the batter, beat in, then fold in the egg white. Coat the parsnips with the batter and deep-fry until puffed-up and golden.

SOUFFLE POTATOES

These pommes soufflées *feature in the repertoire of French* haute cuisine. *They are in effect puffed-up potato chips, golden pillows of potato, their invention was a lucky accident – or so the story goes. A French chef, awaiting the arrival of a distinguished guest, was rather premature with the fried potatoes, so he removed them from the pan and set them aside. Eventually, when the time came to reheat them, the chef plunged them into very hot fat and the chips instantly inflated into crispy balloons.*

When you fry a chipped potato in hot fat, a mass of tiny bubbles rises to the surface as the steam is liberated. The fat gradually seals the surface of the chips, trapping the residual steam inside. If you now remove the chips, and plunge them into fat at a higher temperature, the steam expands and the chips puff up.

As the chef is more or less at the mercy of a random biochemical reaction, there is an inevitable failure rate – about one chip in five fails to perform. Much depends on cutting the chips to the correct size and shape, the temperature of the fat, and the type of potato. Recipes vary, but by experiment I have found the following one successful:

Makes six servings.

	Imperial	Metric	American
Potatoes	2 lb	1 kg	2 lb
Oil for frying			

Choose baking potatoes: King Edward, Desirée or Red Kings are suitable. Slice the potatoes as evenly as possible into slices, ⅜″ (75 mm), and no thinner. Trim into ovals about 2″ (5 cm) across, or cut into oblongs and trim off the corners.

You will need a cook's thermometer, and a deep-fat fryer, or ideally an electric fryer with a graduated temperature scale. Bring the fat to between 150° C–160° C/300° F–325° F and lower the chips in. They will sink to the bottom, but will rise to the surface after 40–50 seconds. For the first few minutes they will frizz madly, then settle down to a more benign state and will turn golden. Let them cook for 5 to 6 minutes, you will notice that blisters begin to form, some chips may even start to balloon at this stage.

Remove them onto a dish. Set the temperature up to 190° C–200° C/375° F–400° F and plunge the chips in. They will puff up immediately. It is best to make an experimental batch; you can, in fact, re-fry them for a few seconds in very hot fat before serving. Serve dredged with salt.

GRATIN DAUPHINOIS

The most popular of baked-potato dishes, although experts fail to agree on the authentic ingredients. Some say no cheese – others say cheese but specify the Gruyère de Comte.

Makes four servings.

	Imperial	Metric	American
Potatoes	1 lb	450 g	1 lb
Garlic clove – 1			
Butter	1 oz	30 g	2 tbsp
Salt and pepper			
Nutmeg			
Cheese, either Gruyère or Cheddar, optional	2–3 oz	55–85 g	2–3 oz
Egg – 1			
Cream	2 tbsp	2 tbsp	3 tbsp
Milk	10 fl oz	275 ml	1¼ cups

Preheat oven to 180° C/350° F/Gas Mark 4.

Peel and finely slice the potatoes about ⅛″ (25 mm) thick – easy if you have a mandolin. Take an oven-proof dish, such as a pyrex of suitable capacity, rub the inside with a cut clove of garlic, and smear a little butter. Arrange layers of potato with sprinklings of salt, black pepper and nutmeg. Add grated cheese if you wish. Beat the egg with the cream and milk. Pour over the potatoes and dot with butter. Bake for 1 hour, or until nicely browned on top.

Serve with a main course.

PEAR AND ALMOND TART

To make 1 × 9″ (23 cm) tart (pie shell).

FOR THE FILLING

	Imperial	Metric	American
William pears, peeled, halved and cored – 4			
Red wine	4 fl oz	115 ml	½ cup
Sugar	2 oz	55 g	4 tbsp
Scarlet food colouring – 1 dash			
Softened butter	4 oz	115 g	½ cup
Castor (fine granulated) sugar	4 oz	115 g	½ cup
Ground almonds	4 oz	115 g	1 cup
Eggs – 2			
Rum	2 fl oz	55 ml	¼ cup
Apricot jam or sugar syrup			

FOR THE PASTRY

	Imperial	Metric	American
Plain (all purpose) flour	5 oz	140 g	1¼ cups
Chilled butter	3 oz	85 g	6 tbsp
Castor (fine granulated) sugar	2 oz	55 g	4 tbsp
Egg yolk – 1			
Iced water	3 tbsp	3 tbsp	Scant ¼ cup

Poach the pear halves in a light syrup made with enough water to cover the sugar and red wine – about a wineglass should suffice. Add a dash of scarlet food colouring for extra colour. Cook for about 25 minutes, or until soft, depending on the ripeness of the pears. Leave to cool, and drain thoroughly.

Rub in the fat, the sugar, then the egg yolk mixed with iced water to form a dough. Allow to rest. Roll out to fit a 9″ (23 cm) tart or flan (pie shell) dish, leave to rest in the refrigerator.

Preheat the oven to 200° C/400° F/Gas Mark 6.

Put the butter into a mixing bowl with the remainder of the sugar and beat until light. Add ground almonds, the eggs and the rum, blending all together.

Spoon two-thirds into the unbaked shell, spread evenly. Press pear halves concentrically around the shell, into the mixture. Fill gaps with remaining mixture. Bake for 30 minutes. Cool, then glaze fruit with heated apricot jam or sugar syrup.

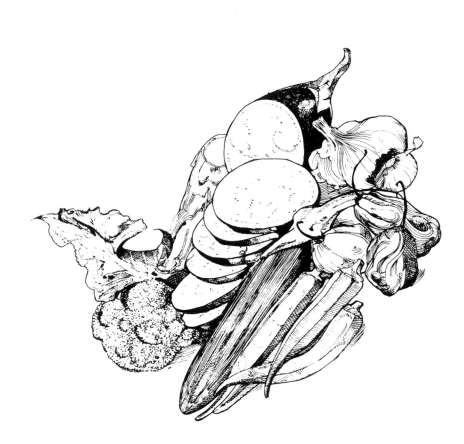

SAVOY PEARS

*Baked pears in a creamy sauce. Choose for preference Comice pears or Packham's
Triumph, and fruit that is firm or just underripe.*
    Makes four servings.

	Imperial	Metric	American
Pears – 4			
Butter	2 oz	50 g	¼ cup
Sugar	4 oz	115 g	½ cup
Single (coffee) cream	3 tbsp	3 tbsp	Scant ¼ cup

Preheat oven to 190° C/375° F/Gas Mark 5.
    Peel, halve and core the pears. Put them in a heatproof dish, cover with sugar
and small pieces of butter. Bake them for 1 hour, or until tender, basting with the
syrup now and then. Put the dish on the top shelf of the oven, and turn up to
maximum heat to burn and caramelise the pears. Add the cream, which will
bubble and make a sauce. Serve hot.

BAKED FRESH FIGS

Makes one serving.

	Imperial	Metric	American
Fresh figs/person – 2			
Brown sugar	2 tbsp	2 tbsp	3 tbsp
Water	1 tbsp	1 tbsp	1 tbsp
Cream to serve			

Preheat oven to 180° C/350° F/Gas Mark 4.

A simple but delicious way of serving fresh figs, allow 2 figs per person. Put them in an oven-proof dish, sprinkle well with brown sugar, and also a little water. Bake in a moderate oven until the sugar and juices from the figs have formed a red sauce. Leave them to get cold, and serve with thick cream.

APPLE CHARLOTTE

There are several versions of this popular fruit pudding, one version has bread tailored to fit a mould, and filled with apple puree; others have apple puree layered with butter-fried crumbs. Then there's the Brown Betty type, with layers of sliced bread, fruit and brown sugar. To make the moulded, free-standing version you will need:

Makes 6 servings.

	Imperial	Metric	American
Butter	4 oz	115 g	½ cup
Stale white bread, not a sliced loaf – 1 loaf			
Medium-sized Bramley apples – 6 or 7			
Sugar	8 oz	225 g	1 cup
FOR THE SAUCE			
Apricot jam	6 oz	170 g	½ cup
Rum	1 tsp	1 tsp	1 tsp
Water	1 tbsp	1 tbsp	1 tbsp

You will need a 6″ (15 cm) diameter charlotte mould or pudding basin (oven-proof bowl).

Cut a circle of greaseproof (wax) paper to fit the bottom of the mould. Butter the paper and sides of the mould and sprinkle with a little sugar. Cut the bread into slices about ¼″ (50 mm) thick. Cut a circle of bread to fit the bottom, or six triangles to make the circle. Cut rectangles to line the sides, each to the depth of the mould. Melt butter in the pan and coat each slice on both sides. Line the mould with rectangles so that they slightly overlap. Make sure there are no gaps or holes (if you don't do this the puree will burst through the seams as you unmould the pudding).

Peel and slice the apples, cook with the sugar and as little water as possible in a suitable pan, stirring frequently to get a thick puree. Leave to cool.

Preheat oven to 190° C/375° F/Gas Mark 5.

Fill the mould with the puree, cover the top with the tailored bread slices, also dipped in butter. Cover the mould and bake on the middle shelf of the oven for 50 minutes. Allow to rest for 20 minutes before gently sliding a knife blade around the pudding, and inverting it onto a serving dish.

Sprinkle a little sugar over the pudding and glaze under a very hot grill. Apple charlotte is usually served with a sauce made with apricot jam, thinned with a little water and flavoured with rum.

PUMPKIN PIE

Makes 1 × 9″ (23 cm) pie.

FOR THE PASTRY

	Imperial	Metric	American
Plain (all purpose) flour	6 oz	170 g	1½ cups
Chilled butter	4 oz	115 g	½ cup
Castor (fine granulated) sugar	1 tbsp	1 tbsp	1 tbsp
Iced water	4–5 tbsp	4–5 tbsp	5–6 tbsp

FOR THE FILLING

	Imperial	Metric	American
Pumpkin	2½–3 lb	1–1½ kg	2½–3 lb
which will yield:	1½ lb	700 g	1½ lb
and make a puree of:	1 pint	600 ml	2½ cups
Brown muscovado sugar	6 oz	170 g	¾ cup
Ginger	½ tsp	½ tsp	½ tsp
Ground cloves	½ tsp	½ tsp	½ tsp
Ground cinnamon	1 tsp	1 tsp	1 tsp
Eggs – 2			
Double (whipping) cream	5 fl oz	150 ml	⅔ cup
Applejack or Calvados	1 tbsp	1 tbsp	1 tbsp

Rub butter into the flour to a texture of breadcrumbs, add sugar, then iced water. Form a dough, roll out and line a 9″ (23 cm) flan (pie shell) dish. Leave to rest.

Preheat oven to 180° C/350° F/Gas Mark 4.

Remove rinds, seeds and stringy bits of pumpkin, cut into matchbox-size cubes. Boil in water for 10–15 minutes until soft. Mash, or pass through sieve to make a puree. Add brown sugar, spices, beaten eggs and cream to make a smooth batter.

Pour batter into dish and bake for about 45 minutes. Test with a fine skewer to see if batter is set. Serve lukewarm.

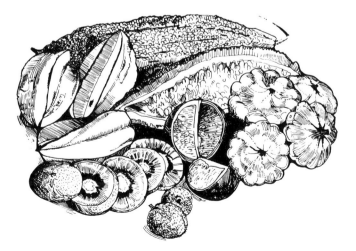

PUMPKIN MARMALADE

This recipe requires some dedication if you haven't got a food processor to slice the pumpkin.

   To make 4 × 1 lb (450 g) jars.

	Imperial	Metric	American
Pumpkin, approx.	4 lb	2 kg	4 lb
Yields:	2½ lb	1½ kg	2½ lb
Preserving sugar	2 lb	1 kg	4½ cups
Lemons – 2			
Certo (commercial pectin) as required			

First, remove peel and seeds from the pumpkin and cut into thumb-size pieces. Use a potato peeler to cut wafers of pumpkin the size of a small coin – this can take you 45 minutes – and put into a 12 pint/7 litre/7 quart preserving pan or very large stewpan. Add the preserving sugar. Cut the pith from the lemon peel and then cut it into very fine strips. The sugar will slowly dissolve and the pumpkin will shed water, so leave overnight.

   The next day, squeeze the juice from the lemons and add to the pumpkin. Add sufficient pectin, according to manufacturer's directions. Bring to the boil and simmer for about 30 minutes, then test for set. Even though you may possess a thermometer, it is important to test by pouring a spoonful into a saucer of cold water until the jam gels. Pour the marmalade into clean jam jars.

CHERRY BLINTZES

Makes four servings.

	Imperial	Metric	American
Milk	½ pint	300 ml	1¼ cups
Plain (all purpose) flour	4 oz	115 g	1 cup
Egg – 1			
Oil – few drops/each crepe			
Butter for frying – as required			
Cornflour (cornstarch)	1 tbsp	1 tbsp	1 tbsp
Black cherries – 1 can			
Castor (fine granulated) sugar	4 tbsp	4 tbsp	5 tbsp
Cinnamon	1 tsp	1 tsp	1 tsp
Soured (cultured sour) cream to serve	5 fl oz	125 ml	⅔ cup

TO MAKE THE BATTER

Gradually add half the milk to the plain (all purpose) flour, to make a smooth paste. Add the egg, beat well, and thin down with remaining milk. It should be like thin cream. Put a few drops of oil in a frying pan, and get it really hot. Pour enough batter into the pan to make a *crepe*. If batter seems too thick, and does not easily cover the pan, add a little more milk or water. You should have enough batter to make about eight *crepes*. Flip them over as they cook, and stack them on a plate to one side.

TO MAKE THE FILLING

Take the cornflour (cornstarch) and make a smooth paste with some of the cherry syrup. Blend in the remaining syrup and bring to the boil, stirring as it thickens. Simmer for a minute or two, to cook the flour. Chop the cherries roughly and add to the syrup. Pour a tablespoonful of the filling along the centre of each *crepe*, fold over ends and roll up like a swiss roll.

Fry each blintz – first they were *crepes* or pancakes, now they're blintzes! – in butter for two or three minutes, gently turning them over. Dust with fine sugar and cinnamon. Serve with soured cream.

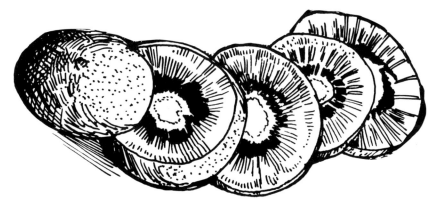

TARTE TATIN

To make 1 × 9″ (23 cm) Tart.

FOR THE PASTRY

	Imperial	Metric	American
Plain (all purpose) flour	5 oz	150 g	1¼ cups
Butter	3 oz	75 g	⅓ cup
Castor (fine granulated) sugar	2 oz	50 g	¼ cup
Ground almonds	1 oz	30 g	¼ cup
Egg yolk – 1			
Water	1 tbsp	1 tbsp	1 tbsp

FOR THE FILLING

	Imperial	Metric	American
Crisp dessert apples such as Granny Smith – 8			
Butter	5 oz	150 g	⅔ cup
Sugar	6 oz	175 g	¾ cup
Water	2 tbsp	2 tbsp	3 tbsp
Cinnamon – a sprinkling			
Cream to serve			

TO MAKE THE PASTRY

Rub the butter into the flour. Add the sugar, almonds and egg yolk and water. Mix to a stiff dough, wrap in cling-film and leave to rest for an hour. Use a 9″ (23 cm) tart or flan (pie shell) dish and butter it well.

TO MAKE THE FILLING

Peel the apples, quarter and core them, then cut each quarter lengthwise. Melt butter in a frying pan, add the sugar and the 2 tablespoons of water. Stir over a high heat for 2 minutes until sugar has melted – it must not caramelise. Quickly add apples and turn them over in the bubbling syrup. After about 7 minutes the apples will have softened but will still retain their shape. Transfer apple pieces to the tart (pie shell) dish, leaving syrup behind, and arrange pieces concentrically. Pile remaining apples on top and dust with cinnamon. Return pan to the heat and boil until the syrup bubbles thickly and turns a toffee colour. Pour over the apples and leave to cool for 1 hour.

Preheat oven to 180° C/350° F/Gas Mark 4.

Roll out pastry in a circle slightly larger than the dish, drape it over your rolling pin, and transfer it carefully (as it is very crumbly and liable to break), then lay it over the apples. Trim, and push edges of pastry well down around the rim of the dish to seal in the apples. Use any trimmings and pack these in as well. Make a slit in the top, and bake on the middle shelf for 25 minutes.

Leave for 10 minutes to cool, then invert the tart onto a serving dish so the apples are uppermost. The tart should be served slightly warm, with thick cream.

PICKLED ONIONS

	Imperial	Metric	American
Pickling onions	2 lb	900 g	2 lb
Coarse salt	2 oz	55 g	2 oz
Pickling spice	3 tsp	3 tsp	3 tsp
Malt vinegar	1½ pints	850 ml	3¾ cups
Sugar	4 oz	115 g	½ cup
Whole cloves – 6			
Black peppercorns	1 tsp	1 tsp	1 tsp

Peel the onions, blanch them in boiling water for 1–2 minutes, then plunge into cold water. Drain, sprinkle with salt and stir. Leave overnight.

Rinse the onions and dry them. Put the vinegar, sugar, spices and peppercorns into a pan, bring to the boil and continue cooking for about 5 minutes. Add the onions, boil for a further five minutes.

Pack into dry jars and pour the vinegar/spice mixture to cover, filling jars to within ¼″ (50 mm) of the top. When cold, seal jars and allow at least three weeks before using.

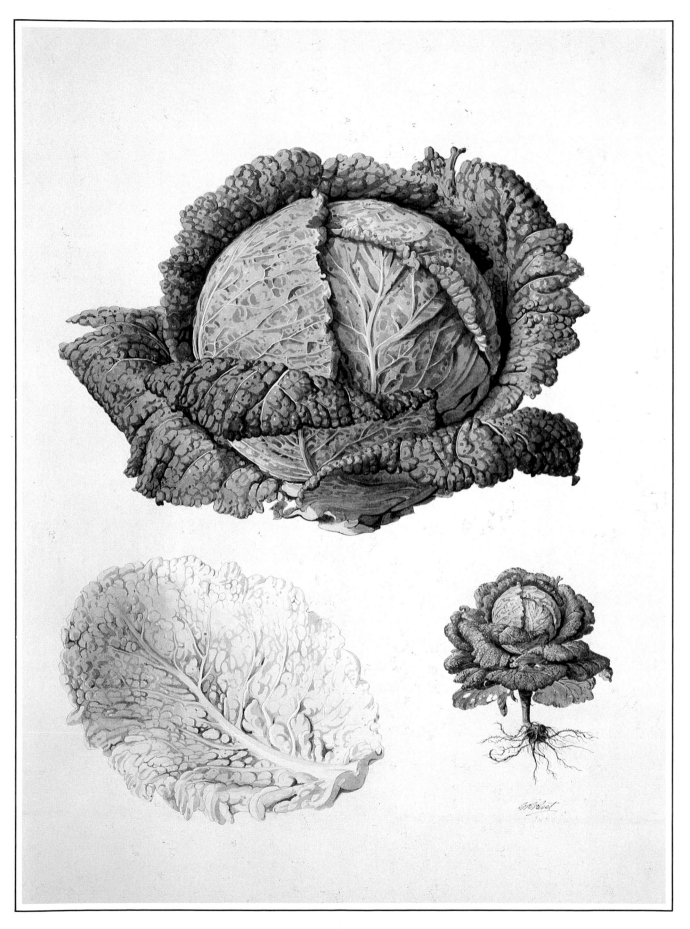

APPLE CHUTNEY

Makes approximately 4½ lbs (2 kg).

	Imperial	Metric	American
Bramley apples	3 lb	1350 g	3 lb
Onions	1 lb	450 g	1 lb
Sultanas	8 oz	225 g	1½ cups
Soft brown sugar	1 lb	450 g	1 lb
Malt vinegar	¾ pint	425 ml	Scant 2 cups
Pickling spice	1 heaped tsp	1 heaped tsp	1 heaped tsp
Grated fresh ginger	1 tsp	1 tsp	1 tsp
Salt	1 tsp	1 tsp	1 tsp
Black pepper	½ tsp	½ tsp	½ tsp

Peel, core and coarsely chop the apples and onions. Put them in a preserving pan with the rest of the ingredients. Bring to the boil, then lower heat and simmer uncovered until the mixture is of a suitably thick consistency – about 2 hours.

Stir from time to time to prevent the mixture from sticking. Leave to cool for 15 minutes before pouring into prepared jars. Cover and label.

WinteR

The store of autumnal fruits and vegetables sustain us through most of winter but the latter also has its own produce heralded by the pumpkins and squashes of November, to be transformed into soups and sweet pies, and lanterns for Halloween. Over the centuries gardeners have evolved a great variety of cabbages. The original plants still grow wild along our coast. Hardy varieties of cauliflowers, Savoy, drumhead and red cabbages, kohlrabi have been developed. Some of our native vegetables do indeed need the nip of frost to bestow flavour and crispness – such as celery, celeriac, Brussels sprouts and parsnips. Look out also for the versatile Jerusalem artichokes.

Around November boxes of scarlet cranberries arrive from America. Discovered by the early settlers, the then wild berries were seen as a substitute for raisins and other fruit. Expatriate Americans snap them up as they are a must for the cranberry sauce for the Thanksgiving turkey. Cranberries are also delicious in pies and puddings.

A whole gamut of citrus fruits brings a touch of colour to the short dark days around Christmas. Look out for chestnuts and other dry fruits as well as the delicious dates which appear at that time.

The month of January sees the arrival of Seville oranges for marmalade; and in the big supermarkets imports of exotic produce from countries in the southern hemisphere are inspiring in their variety: avocados, pineapples, Japanese pears, limes, prickly pears, tangerines and clementines remind us that spring is round the corner.

POTATO AND LEEK SOUP

Makes six servings.

	Imperial	Metric	American
Potatoes	1 lb	450 g	1 lb
Large leeks – 4			
Oil or butter	1 tbsp	1 tbsp	1 tbsp
Milk	1 pint	600 ml	2½ cups
Water	½ pint	300 ml	1¼ cups
Salt and pepper			
Cream	2 tbsp	2 tbsp	3 tbsp

Wash the leeks well under cold running water. Finely slice the white part of the leeks, checking that no soil is trapped between the rings. Sauté them in oil over a gentle heat.

Meanwhile, peel and cut the potatoes into cubes, add to the leeks, and leave them to sweat, stirring from time to time. Add the milk and water and simmer until the potatoes are soft.

Pass the vegetables through a sieve, or puree in a blender, return to the pan, and season to taste. The addition of a little cream enriches this 'peasant' soup.

The addition of a lot of cream and chopped chives, makes a CREME VICHYS-SOISE, a favourite summer soup invariably served well chilled.

PUMPKIN SOUP

Makes four servings.

	Imperial	Metric	American
Pumpkin, peeled	1 lb	450 g	1 lb
Butter	1 oz	30 g	2 tbsp
Small onion – 1			
Milk, approx.	¾ pint	425 ml	Scant pint
Cream, approx.	3 fl oz	75 ml	generous ⅓ cup
Salt and pepper			
Lemon juice	1 tsp	1 tsp	1 tsp
Nutmeg, optional – 1 pinch			

Boil pumpkin in a little water until soft (about 15 minutes). Drain well. Heat butter, add chopped onion and stew until soft. Add pumpkin and leave to sweat for about 5 minutes over a gentle heat.

Put in blender, or through a sieve to make a fine puree. Add milk and cream – the quantity you use depends on how thick and rich you want the soup to be, but pumpkin soup should be smooth, creamy and golden in colour.

Flavour with salt, white pepper and a squeeze of lemon juice. Some cooks add a grating of nutmeg. Serve with crunchy bread croûtons.

BLACK LENTIL SOUP

Makes four servings.

	Imperial	Metric	American
Puy lentils	8 oz	225 g	1 cup
Medium-sized onion – 1			
Garlic clove – 1			
Oil	1 tbsp	1 tbsp	1 tbsp
Crushed or powdered cumin	1 tsp	1 tsp	1 tsp
Tomatoes – 2			
Sugar	1 heaped tsp	1 heaped tsp	1 heaped tsp
Salt and pepper			
Fresh coriander – a few sprigs			
Lemon juice	1 tbsp	1 tbsp	1 tbsp

Wash and pick over lentils, then leave to soak for 30 minutes. Chop onion (use an Italian red onion if you can find any) and mince garlic. Sauté in oil with the cumin until soft.

Plunge tomatoes in boiling water for a few seconds. Remove skins, chop roughly and add to onion. Leave to sweat for about 5 minutes on low heat.

Now add lentils, sugar, salt and pepper, and about 1 pint/600 ml/2½ cups water. Simmer for 40 minutes. Puree two-thirds of the lentils in a blender, or pass through a sieve. Mix with the remaining whole lentils, taste for seasoning. Chop fresh coriander and add with the lemon juice to the soup. Heat before serving.

PALESTINE SOUP

The basis of this soup is the Jerusalem artichoke, and it acquired its name through somewhat tortuous associations. The plant is a member of the sunflower family. Sunflower is girasole *in Italian, hence* girasole – 'Jerusalem' to the English ear, leads us to 'Palestine'. The French, marginally less addicted to puns, avoid the whole thing by calling the vegetable topinambour.

Botanically it is a tuber, and was once thought to taste like artichoke bottoms; the only thing the vegetables have in common is that they do not easily yield their edible heart. Jerusalem artichokes are tricky to peel because they are so irregular and knobbly. The best way is to boil them until just tender, plunge them into cold water, then peel away the skin. As you do this, put them in acidulated water (containing a few drops of lemon juice or vinegar) to prevent them from discolouring.

Makes eight servings.

	Imperial	Metric	American
Jerusalem artichokes	1 lb	450 g	1 lb
Medium-sized onion – 1			
Celery sticks (stalks) – 2 or 3			
Butter	1 oz	30 g	2 tbsp
Garlic clove – half			
Milk and water, mixed equally	¾ pint	425 ml	Scant 2 cups
Nutmeg	¼ tsp	¼ tsp	¼ tsp
Single (coffee) cream	1 tbsp	1 tbsp	1 tbsp
Salt to taste			
Lemon juice	1 tsp	1 tsp	1 tsp
Chopped parsley for decoration			

Prepare the artichokes as described above. Finely chop the onion and the celery then sauté in the heated butter until soft. Peel the artichokes and add to the onion. Stir-fry for a minute or two, then add half a clove of minced garlic, the milk/water mixture and a little grated nutmeg. Simmer for 10 minutes, then puree the soup in a blender or press through a fine sieve.

Stir in the cream, and add salt to taste, and the lemon juice. The soup should be smooth and white. If you like, stir in a swirl of cream into each bowl just before serving, and sprinkle with chopped parsley. Croûtons of white bread may also be served.

BLACK BEAN SOUP

A creamy puree of beans, flavoured with garlic.
    Makes four servings.

	Imperial	Metric	American
Small black beans	1 lb	450 g	1 lb
Garlic – 4 cloves			
Water, approx.	1 pint	570 ml	2½ cups
Single (coffee) cream	5 oz	150 ml	⅔ cup
Salt and black pepper			

Soak beans overnight. Simmer them until tender in the water in which they have soaked – about 30 minutes – together with the peeled cloves of garlic. Puree in a blender, season to taste. Add the cream, return to the heat, keep just below boiling to reheat before serving.

This soup is recommended as a hangover cure, especially if you add a beaten egg before serving.

CELERIAC AND CARROT REMOULADE

Celeriac rémoulade is a popular hors d'oeuvres in Paris bistro cookery. You can, of course, add other vegetables – carrots make a good combination, so do scorzonera and black salsify.

Makes four servings.

	Imperial	Metric	American
Celeriac	8 oz	225 g	½ lb
Acidulated water (with lemon juice or vinegar)			
Carrots	4 oz	115 g	¼ lb

FOR THE SAUCE

Egg yolk – 1			
French mustard	2 tsp	2 tsp	2 tsp
Salt – 1 pinch			
Oil	2 tbsp	2 tbsp	3 tbsp
Gherkins – 2			
Parsley – a few sprigs			
Tarragon – 1 sprig			
Chervil – 1 sprig			

Peel the celeriac, cut into slices, then into matchstick strips. As you slice each batch, put them in acidulated water (lemon juice or a dash of vinegar added to the water) to stop the celeriac going brown. Scrape and slice carrots likewise. Aim to have about two-thirds celeriac to a third carrot strips. Boil them separately in salted water. The carrots will take about 5 minutes. Allow 20–30 minutes for the celeriac which should be cooked but still firm. Drain thoroughly and leave to cool.

To make the SAUCE REMOULADE, prepare a MAYONNAISE (page 67), add a spoonful of mustard, a finely-chopped gherkin, chopped parsley, tarragon and chervil, if you have it. The quantity you make depends on the amount of celeriac you have prepared, but the vegetables should be generously coated in the sauce.

Serve with French bread as a starter.

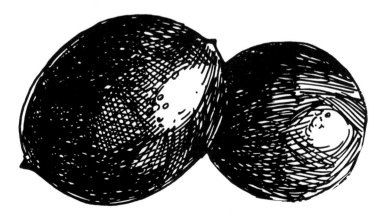

VEGETABLE GRATIN

As with many mixed vegetable dishes, the type of vegetable and the quantity can vary considerably, according to what may be available. For this gratin dish I used the following:

Makes four servings.

	Imperial	Metric	American
Medium-sized onion – 1			
Aubergine (eggplant) – 1			
Carrots – 2			
Celery sticks (stalks) – 3			
Celeriac – 1 slice			
Large courgette (zucchini) – 1			
White radish *mooli* **– 1**			
Medium-sized turnip – 1			
Leeks – 2			
Parsnip – 1			
Eddoes – 2*			
Medium-sized potatoes – 2			
Tin of tomatoes	1 × 14 oz	1 × 400 g	1 × 14 oz
Garlic clove – 1			
Bay leaf – 1			
Pistou sauce (page 47)	1 heaped tbsp	1 heaped tbsp	1 heaped tbsp
Salt and pepper			
Breadcrumbs, dried	1 oz	30 g	¼ cup
Small piece of lemon rind			

*Chinese vegetable

Preheat oven to 180° C/350° F/Gas Mark 4.

Prepare the vegetables accordingly: peel and dice potatoes, trim, wash and chop leeks, peel turnip, slice and chop aubergine (eggplant), scrape and dice carrots, chop celeriac etc. The vegetables should be chopped fairly coarsely so as not to lose their identity. Blanch all of them in boiling water for 2 minutes, then plunge into cold water and drain thoroughly. Put in an oven dish with the tomatoes, minced garlic, bay leaf, pistou sauce, salt and pepper. Cover with breadcrumbs and grated lemon rind. Bake for 30 minutes. Sprinkle with chopped parsley just before serving.

STUFFED CHAYOTE

The pale green pear-shaped chayote, cho-cho or christophene, is a member of the gourd or squash family. It has a fugitive, bland flavour and needs some support from other ingredients. In the West Indies it is sometimes curried (boiled, sliced and sautéd in a curry spice mixture), or stuffed with rice. The following recipe uses a mushroom and tarragon filling. Serve as a starter.

Makes four servings.

	Imperial	Metric	American
Chayotes – 2			
Button mushrooms	4 oz	115 g	1 cup
Butter	1–2 oz	30–55 g	2–4 tbsp
Plain (all purpose) flour	1 tbsp	1 tbsp	1 tbsp
Milk	3 fl oz	85 ml	⅓ cup
Cream	1½ tbsp	1½ tbsp	2 tbsp
Tarragon, fresh or dried	1 tsp	1 tsp	1 tsp
Salt and black pepper			
Chopped parsley	1 tbsp	1 tbsp	1 tbsp
Brown breadcrumbs, fresh	1 oz	30 g	½ cup

Peel the chayotes, cut them in half, and scoop out the seed and core like a pear, leaving a cavity for stuffing (you can eat the nut-like seeds). Put the halves into cold water in a pan, bring to the boil, and simmer for 45 minutes or until they are tender, but not soft. Drain. Trim the bottoms so that they stand upright.

Preheat oven to 180° C/350° F/Gas Mark 4.

Make the stuffing with the finely-chopped mushrooms sautéd in the butter. Add the flour, stir, and add the milk by degrees to make a thick sauce. Add the cream, the tarragon, salt and pepper to taste. Mix the parsley with the bread-crumbs, and add half the mixture to the sauce.

Fill the cavities with the mixture, and press the remaining crumbs on top. Trickle a spoonful of oil or melted butter over the chayotes, and bake for 30 minutes, or until nicely browned. The stuffed chayotes can be served hot or cold.

SWEET POTATO PUREE

Makes two servings.

	Imperial	Metric	American
Sweet potatoes	1 lb	450 g	1 lb
Single (coffee) cream	2 tbsp	2 tbsp	3 tbsp
Dry sherry	1 tbsp	1 tbsp	1 tbsp
Butter	1–2 oz	30–55 g	2–4 tbsp
Salt			
Nutmeg	¼ tsp	¼ tsp	¼ tsp
Chopped parsley			

Preheat oven to 180° C/350° F/Gas Mark 4.

Bake the potatoes until tender. Peel, puree with the cream, sherry and two thirds of the butter. Add salt to taste and nutmeg. Put in an ovenware dish, dot with butter, and bake for 20 minutes. Serve scattered with chopped parsley.

ALIGOT

A potato and cheese puree from the Auvergne in France, using Tomme de Cantal cheese. You can replace the Cantal with Gruyère, or even Cheddar. The puree is enriched with cream, milk and butter, and has garlic as an additional flavour. Served with bread, aligot is practically a meal in itself.

Makes four servings.

	Imperial	Metric	American
Potatoes	1 lb	450 g	1 lb
Cheese	4 oz	115 g	¼ lb
Cream	4 fl oz	125 ml	½ cup
Milk, more if required	2 fl oz	55 ml	¼ cup
Butter	2 oz	55 g	4 tbsp
Garlic clove – 1			
Salt and pepper			
Parsley, optional	1 tbsp	1 tbsp	1 tbsp

Boil the potatoes, then mash to a puree, adding the milk, cream and butter to obtain a creamy smooth consistency. Keep on a low heat, then add grated cheese, stirring vigorously. It should be thick and rich, but add milk as you require. Crush the garlic clove into the puree and add salt and black pepper to taste. Some cooks also add finely-chopped parsley.

BRAISED RED CABBAGE WITH CHESTNUTS AND APPLES

Makes four servings.

	Imperial	Metric	American
Chestnuts	8 oz	225 g	½ lb
Onion – 1			
Medium-sized red cabbage – 1	1 lb–1½ lb	½–¾ kg	1½ lb
Russet apples – 2			
Salt and pepper			
Grated nutmeg	¼ tsp	¼ tsp	¼ tsp
Oil	2 tbsp	2 tbsp	3 tbsp
Lemon juice or vinegar	2 tbsp	2 tbsp	3 tbsp
Water	½ pint	300 ml	1¼ cups

Preheat oven to 160° C/325° F/Gas Mark 3.

Boil the chestnuts for 5 minutes, peel away shells, then grill to remove skins. Chop coarsely.

Finely slice onion and fry in heated oil until soft. Finely slice cabbage, discarding thick stalks, and stir-fry with the onion. Core and rough-chop apples, add to the cabbage along with the nuts. Season with salt, pepper and nutmeg.

Put cabbage mixture in a casserole, add lemon juice and water, cover and braise in the oven for about 2 hours. Check now and again to see that the cabbage is moist, add more water if it is drying out. The lemon juice helps to preserve the red colour of the cabbage. You can use vinegar as an alternative.

CELERIAC PUREE

Makes four servings.

	Imperial	Metric	American
Celeriac	1 lb	459 g	1 lb
Potatoes	1 lb	450 g	1 lb
Olive oil	1 tbsp	1 tbsp	1 tbsp
Cream	2–3 tbsp	2–3 tbsp	3–4 tbsp
Salt and pepper			

Boil the potatoes in their skins. Peel, slice and boil the celeriac in a little water (it may take as long as 1 hour to tenderise), or cook in a steamer. Peel potatoes, mash to a fine puree with the celeriac, oil and cream, adding salt and pepper to taste.

This is a rich mixture – the more oil and cream you add the smoother it becomes.

Serve as an accompaniment to a main dish. It goes particularly well with grilled or baked white fish.

AMERICAN FRIED CABBAGE

White, or Dutch cabbage, stir-fried with chopped onion, sugar and spices.
Makes four servings.

	Imperial	Metric	American
Cabbage – 1			
Oil	1 tbsp	1 tbsp	1 tbsp
Spanish onion – 1			
Sugar	1 tbsp	1 tbsp	1 tbsp
Vinegar	1 tbsp	1 tbsp	1 tbsp
Cinnamon	1 tsp	1 tsp	1 tsp
Nutmeg – 1 pinch			
Water	5 fl oz	150 ml	⅔ cup

Slice onion finely and sauté in heated oil. Add finely-sliced cabbage, and stir-fry for 5 minutes. Dissolve sugar in hot water, add spices and vinegar, pour over the cabbage, cover and simmer until the liquid has reduced to about 1 tablespoonful – it will take about 15 minutes.

Serve with a main dish.

BRAISED CHICORY

The plump, white shoots tipped with yellow were first grown in Belgium during the 19th century, where they are known as witloof. *To us they are 'chicory', while the French and Americans call them 'endive'. They are widely used as a salad vegetable, but they are excellent when braised, to accompany a main dish of meat or fish.*

Makes four servings.

	Imperial	Metric	American
Chicory (endive) shoots – 8			
Butter	2 oz	55 g	¼ cup
Lemon juice	1 tbsp	1 tbsp	1 tbsp
Dry white wine	4 fl oz	115 ml	½ cup
Salt and black pepper			
Parsley – a few sprigs			

Preheat oven to 180° C/350° F/Gas Mark 4.

Blanch the chicory (endive) in boiling water for 5 minutes, then refresh with cold water. Drain thoroughly, and arrange in a suitable oven-proof dish.

Pour the wine over the chicory (endive), dot with butter and season with salt and pepper. Cover the dish, and cook in a moderate oven until tender. This will take approximately 30 minutes. Drain the liquid, reduce in a small pan, and pour over the chicory (endive). Sprinkle with a little chopped parsley before serving.

JERUSALEM ARTICHOKES IN MUSTARD SAUCE

This is a nice way of preparing Jerusalem artichokes, but it is fair to point out that the old cookery books were correct when they charged this vegetable with 'provoking ill humours and wind' – at least, the latter part of the statement is undoubtedly true.

Makes four servings.

	Imperial	Metric	American
Jerusalem artichokes	1 lb	450 g	1 lb
FOR THE SAUCE			
Plain (all purpose) flour	1 tbsp	1 tbsp	1 tbsp
Butter	1 oz	30 g	2 tbsp
Milk	6–8 fl oz	170–225 ml	¾–1 cup
French mustard	1 heaped tsp	1 heaped tsp	1 heaped tsp
Chopped parsley	1 tbsp	1 tbsp	1 tbsp

Wash the artichokes and boil them for 10 minutes. Plunge into cold water, then peel away the skin. Drop them into water with a dash of vinegar or lemon juice. Bring to the boil and simmer until tender.

Make a roux by melting the butter and adding the flour. Stir, then gradually add enough milk to obtain a smooth sauce. Add the mustard, then taste for seasoning. Pour the sauce over the artichokes in a heatproof serving dish, and glaze for a few moments under a hot grill. Sprinkle with parsley and serve with a main course.

POMMES DE TERRE ANNA

An attractive potato cake made from shaped and thinly-sliced potato, cooked in butter.

Makes four servings.

	Imperial	Metric	American
Potatoes	1 lb	450 g	1 lb
Butter	2–3 oz	55–85 g	¼–⅓ cup
Salt and pepper			
Chopped parsley			

Preheat oven to 180° C/350° F/Gas Mark 4.

There are two methods of preparing this dish. One is in a casserole in the oven, the other in a frying pan on top of the stove. Peel the potatoes uniformly, or trim them to make cylinders of equal size. Slice them thinly, preferably on a mandolin, and pat them dry.

Melt the butter. Brush the base of a casserole dish with some of the butter, arrange the potato slices, in a circle, with the slices overlapping until you have covered the bottom of the dish. Season with salt and pepper, trickle some of the butter on top, then arrange a second layer. Continue in this way until all the slices are used up.

Put a lid on the casserole, and bake in the oven for 30 minutes, or until the potatoes are soft, and the underside browned. Invert onto a serving dish.

If you adopt the second cooking method, arrange the slices in the frying pan, as above, and sauté until brown. Then – with care – turn the potato cake upside down and brown the other side. Serve, sprinkled with chopped parsley, to accompany a main dish.

VEGETABLE PUREE

This is a white puree, made with potatoes, celeriac, leeks, turnips and Jerusalem artichokes.

Makes four servings.

	Imperial	Metric	American
Medium-sized potatoes – 2			
Leeks – 3			
Celeriac	12 oz–1 lb	340–450 g	¾ lb–1 lb
Jerusalem artichokes	8 oz	225 g	½ lb
Small turnips – 3			
Garlic clove – 1			
Butter	2 oz	55 g	¼ cup
Single (coffee) cream	5 fl oz	150 ml	⅔ cup
Bay leaf – 1			
Peppercorns – 4			
Bouquet garni of parsley, oregano and thyme – 1			
Salt			

Prepare the vegetables and slice quite thinly to facilitate rapid cooking. Add the garlic in one piece, the bay leaf and peppercorns, the bouquet garni wrapped in a piece of muslin. Boil until tender (about 20 minutes).

Drain and puree in a blender or liquidiser. Return to the pan, add the butter and cream and stir over a low flame until you get a smooth, creamy puree. Taste for seasoning and serve hot with a main dish.

SPINACH TART

Bailey's (no relation) Household Dictionary of 1736 gives a recipe for 'A Spinage Tart' sweetened with sugar and flavoured with rosewater and ground almonds. It was latticed on the top, and closely resembled the French spinach tart, still baked at Christmas-time in Provence – a rather startling-looking dessert, strewn with candied peel and with a rich green filling – it tastes not unlike pumpkin pie.

To make 1 × 9″ (23 cm) tart (pie shell).

FOR THE PASTRY

	Imperial	Metric	American
Plain (all purpose) flour	6 oz	170 g	1½ cups
Chilled butter	4½ oz	130 g	Generous ½ cup
Iced water	4 tbsp	4 tbsp	5 tbsp
Salt – 1 pinch			

FOR THE FILLING

	Imperial	Metric	American
Finely-chopped or pureed spinach	6 oz	170 g	¾ cup
Sugar	4 oz	115 g	½ cup
Mixed cream and milk, in equal quantities	15 fl oz	425 ml	Scant pint
Grated lemon rind – 1			
Plain (all purpose) flour	1 oz	30 g	¼ cup
Milk	2 tbsp	2 tbsp	3 tbsp
Eggs – 2			
Candied peel – a sprinkling			
Vanilla pod, sugar or essence			
Whipped cream to serve			

TO MAKE THE PASTRY

Chop butter into small pieces and rub into the flour to the consistency of breadcrumbs. Add iced water and form into a dough. Leave to rest for an hour.

Preheat oven to 200° C/400° F/Gas Mark 6.

Roll out the dough to fit a 9″ (23 cm) flan or tart (pie shell) dish, keeping the pastry trimmings. Prick the bottom of the flan with a skewer. To prevent the sides collapsing, shore up with bread crusts. Bake blind (with greaseproof (wax) paper and baking beans) for 5 minutes.

TO MAKE THE FILLING

Wash the spinach and cook to a puree. Bring the milk/cream mixture to the boil with the sugar, lemon rind and vanilla. Make a thin paste with the flour mixed with the additional milk. Separate 1 egg, add yolk to flour paste with whole beaten egg, then blend in with the milk/cream mixture. Cook gently, stirring until the cream thickens, then mix with spinach. If you have a blender, use it for a smoother texture. Allow to cool. Lower oven to 190° C/375° F/Gas Mark 5.

Now pour filling into the pastry case. Roll out trimmings, cut into strips and make a latticed top to the tart. Sprinkle all over with candied peel. Bake for 25 minutes. Serve warm with whipped cream.

ITALIAN BROCCOLI

A quick and simple dish using either broccoli or calabrese.
Makes four servings.

	Imperial	Metric	American
Broccoli	1 lb	450 g	1 lb
Olive oil	1 tbsp	1 tbsp	1 tbsp
Garlic clove – half			
Stoned black olives – 12			

Break the broccoli into flowerets and plunge into boiling water. Cook 4 or 5 minutes until *al dente*.

Put the oil in a pan, and bring to a high heat. Drain broccoli thoroughly and stir-fry in the hot oil. Add a little minced garlic and the olives, roughly-chopped.

Serve with a main course.

APPLES BERRICHONNE

A rich dessert of candied apples, cooked for hours in sugar syrup.
Makes four servings.

	Imperial	Metric	American
Firm dessert apples, such as Granny Smiths – 4			
Sugar	8 oz	225 g	1 cup
Water	8 fl oz	225 ml	1 cup
Rum	1 tbsp	1 tbsp	1 tbsp
Chopped candied peel	2 tsp	2 tsp	2 tsp
Double (whipping) cream	5 fl oz	150 ml	⅔ cup

Quarter and core, but do not peel the apples. Dissolve sugar in the water, add the apple quarters, cover with a loose-fitting lid and simmer over a very low heat for 4–5 hours, until the apples are impregnated with the syrup, and partially crystallised. Prick with a fork, and pour the rum over them. Cool and place in the refrigerator, preferably overnight.

Transfer very carefully to a serving dish and sprinkle with the candied peel. The apples can be served with whipped cream or a thick CREME ANGLAISE which is made by dissolving 1 tablespoon of sugar into ½ pint/300 ml/1¼ cups of milk. Bring this to the boil with a vanilla pod or a few drops of vanilla essence. Allow to cool slightly.

Beat 2 egg yolks. Pour the milk over them, beat thoroughly and pour the mixture into the top of a double-boiler. Stir continuously until the *crème* thickens. Do *not* allow to boil or it will curdle. If you do not have a double-boiler, cook over a very low heat or hold the mixture in a smaller pan into a pot of boiling water.

CRANBERRY SORBET

A true wintertime fruit, usually imported around Christmas for cooks who like fresh cranberry sauce with their turkey. Cranberries are a New England speciality, where they are much appreciated for their sharp, tart quality. New Englanders make cranberry relishes, cranberry muffins, cranberry chiffon pie, and a popular lattice tart. This cranberry sorbet can be served between courses, or as a dessert in hollowed-out fruits such as mangoes or papaya.

Makes four to six servings.

	Imperial	Metric	American
Fresh cranberries	8 oz	225 g	½ lb
Water	½ pint	300 ml	1¼ cups
Granulated sugar	8 oz	225 g	1 cup
Castor (fine granulated) sugar	3 oz	85 g	½ cup
Egg whites – 2			

Boil the berries in ½ pint/300 ml/1¼ cups of water until they pop (2–3 minutes). Press through a sieve, or put in a blender to obtain a puree. Top up with enough water to make ½ pint/300 ml/1¼ cups puree. Sieve to get rid of the pips and skins.

Put 8 fl oz/225 ml/1 cup water in a saucepan, add granulated sugar and stir over the heat until sugar has dissolved. Now bring to the boil and boil for exactly 1 minute. Add this syrup to the puree. Leave to cool, place in a suitable container and freeze in the ice-making compartment of your refrigerator. Stir now and then to prevent ice-crystals forming. When nearly set, whip egg whites stiff, fold in the castor sugar, and blend with the cranberry puree. Freeze until firm.

CARROT, NUT AND SWEET POTATO PUDDING

A light, moist, baked pudding without flour. The pudding rises so you will need a bowl of at least 3 pint/1.7 litre/1¾ quarts capacity, otherwise reduce the quantity to suit the size of your largest pudding basin or bowl.
   Makes six servings.

	Imperial	Metric	American
Sweet potato	1 lb	450 g	1 lb
Grated carrot	7 oz	200 g	7 oz
Grated dessert apple	3 oz	85 g	3 oz
Mixed dried fruit	4 oz	115 g	⅔ cup
Ground almonds	5 oz	140 g	1¼ cups
Ground walnuts	2 oz	55 g	½ cup
Mixed spice	1 tsp	1 tsp	1 tsp
Grated rind of 1 orange and 1 lemon			
Butter	½ oz	15 g	1 tbsp
Eggs – 4			
Castor (fine granulated) sugar	8 oz	225 g	1 cup
Sherry	2 tbsp	2 tbsp	3 tbsp

Bake the potato until cooked throughout – about 1 hour – leave to cool, skin and puree through a sieve. Put in a bowl and add the carrot, apple, dried fruit, nuts, spice and grated rind.
   Cut a disc of greaseproof (wax) paper to fit the bottom of your pudding basin, butter it well, also butter the sides of the basin.
   Preheat oven to 140° C/275° F/Gas Mark 1.
   Separate the eggs. Whisk the yolks with the sugar and sherry in a double-boiler over simmering water until light and thick – this is, in fact, a *zabaglione*. Add the carrot/potato mixture. Whip egg whites until stiff and fold in. Pour into the buttered basin, cover with kitchen foil, and bake for 2 hours. Turn out onto a suitable serving dish.
   Remove the greaseproof (wax) paper disc.
   This pudding can be served with a CREME ANGLAISE (page 124) or with a ZABAGLIONE sauce. Make the latter as explained above in the pudding recipe, but use less sugar – 3 oz (85 g) per 3 egg yolks, and 2 tablespoonfuls of sherry.

SEVILLE ORANGE MARMALADE

Makes 8 lb (4 kg) marmalade.

	Imperial	Metric	American
Seville oranges	2 lb	900 g	2 lb
Lemons – 2			
Water	7 pints	4 litres	4 quarts
Preserving sugar	6 lb	2.7 kg	6 lb

Wash and dry fruit. Cut in halves and squeeze out the juice, strain and retain pips. Chop pulp and add to the juice. Separate pith from the peel, chop pith roughly and add to the pips. Shred peel finely (or coarsely if you want chunky-cut marmalade – the sort that bites back . . .) and add to the pulp and juice.

Allow 3½ pints/2 litres/2 quarts of water per 1 lb (450 g) of fruit. Put the pith and pips in a bowl and cover with some of the water. Add the remaining water to the pulp and juice, together with the shredded peel. Leave to soak overnight.

Strain the water in which the pith has soaked and add to the pulp/peel mixture. Tie the pith and pips in a muslin bag. Put the pulp still in the muslin bag into a preserving pan. You now have in the pan: the peel, pulp and juice from the fruit together with some 6 pints/3.5 litres/3½ quarts of water, and the bag of pith and pips. The pith contains much of the pectin which is the setting agent. Boil until the bulk has been reduced by half – 2–3 hours.

Measure the pulp and allow 1¼ lb (550 g) of sugar per 1 lb (450 g) of pulp. Stir until sugar dissolves, bring to the boil, skim as scum rises, then boil until setting point is reached – 20–30 minutes. Longer boiling darkens the marmalade. If the marmalade refuses to set after 30 minutes, add a measure of commercial pectin such as Certo, according to the instructions on the bottle.

To test for setting, drop a little marmalade into a saucer of cold water. When ready, allow marmalade to cool for 10 minutes or so, before carefully pouring into clean, dry jars. You can obtain a darker marmalade by substituting half brown sugar for half the preserving sugar. Put a circle of waxed paper over the surface of the marmalade in each jar, cover with cellophane and secure with an elastic band. Label and date the jars.

THE RECIPES

Aïoli, 68
Aligot, 113
American Fried Cabbage, 115
Apple Charlotte, 93
Apple Chutney, 103
Apples *Berrichonne*, 124
Apricot and Guava Ice-cream, 66
Aubergine Pâté, 22
Aurore Sauce, *see Béchamel* Sauce, 43
Avocado and Tomato Ice-cream, 54
Avocado Dip, 48
Baked fresh Figs, 92
Bananas in Red Wine, 37
Béarnaise Sauce, 43
Béchamel Sauce, 40
Beurre Blanc, 40
Black Bean Soup, 109
Black Lentil Soup, 107
Borscht, 74
Braised Chicory, 116
Braised Leeks or Endives with Olives and Garlic, 27
Braised Red Cabbage with Chestnuts and Apples, 114
Brie and Spinach in Pastry, 17
Brochettes of Vegetables with Satay Sauce, 49
Brouillade de Truffes, 79
Brown Vegetable Stew, 86
Caponata, 84
Carrot, Nut and Sweet Potato Pudding, 126
Celeriac and Carrot *Rémoulade*, 110
Celeriac Puree, 114
Cheese and Onion *Roulade*, 76
Cherry Blintzes, 96
Choron Sauce, *see Béarnaise* Sauce, 43
Coulis de Tomates, 23
Cranberry Sorbet, 125
Cream of Lettuce and Cucumber Soup, 46
Crème Anglaise, *see* Apples *Berrichonne*, 124
Crème St. Germain, 14
Dutch Apple Fritters, 38
Fruit *Brulé*, 66
Fruit Fools, 57
Gratin Dauphinois, 89
Hollandaise Sauce, 44
Imam-Bayildi, 80
Italian Broccoli, 122
Jerusalem Artichokes in Mustard Sauce, 117
Koulabiak with Aubergines, Mushrooms and Cream Cheese, 26
Leek and Potato Quiche, 25
Lemon Tart, 58
Lentil and Rice Pilaff, 51
Lentil Salad, 34
Maltaise Sauce, *see Hollandaise* Sauce, 44
Mange-tout (edible-podded peas) Soup, 15
Mayonnaise, 67
Michon Dauphinois, 85
Morilles à la Crème, *see* Mushrooms on Toast, 77

Mornay Sauce, *see Béchamel* Sauce, 43
Mousseline Sauce, *see Hollandaise* Sauce, 44
Mushrooms on Toast, 77
Onion Tart, 24
Onions *à la Grecque*, 48
Orange and Almond Tart, 35
Orange Tart, 56
Palestine Soup, 108
Paloise Sauce, *see Béarnaise* Sauce, 43
Papaya and Lime Mousse, 36
Parsnip Fritters, 87
Pasha, 39
Pavlova Cake, 63
Peach Melba, 55
Peaches *à la Diable*, 62
Pear and Almond Tart, 90
Pêches au Cointreau, 55
Pêches Cardinal, 55
Pêches Dame-Blanche, 55
Pepper Salad, 54
Petite Entrée du Jardin, 16
Pickled Onions, 98
Pistou Sauce, *see Pistou* Soup, 47
Pistou Soup, 46
Pommes de Terre Anna, 118
Potato and Leek Soup, 105
Pumpkin Marmalade, 95
Pumpkin Pie, 94
Pumpkin Soup, 106
Ratatouille, 50
Rice and Vegetable Pilaff, 52
Salad of New Potatoes and Herbs, 33
Sauce *Indienne*, *see* Mayonnaise, 67
Sauce *Rémoulade*, *see*, Celeriac and Carrot *Rémoulade*, 108
Sauce Rouille, *see Aïoli*, 68
Sauce Tartare, *see* Mayonnaise, 67
Sauce Verte, *see* Mayonnaise, 67
Savoy Pears, 91
Seville Orange Marmalade, 127
Soufflé Potatoes, 88
Spinach Tart, 123
Spring Vegetables with Pasta, 21
Strawberry Ice Profiteroles, 61
Stuffed Artichoke Bottoms with Avocado, 18
Stuffed Cabbage *à la Turque*, 83
Stuffed Chayote, 112
Summer Pudding, 64
Sweet 'n' Hot Corn and Okra Chowder, 75
Sweet Potato Puree, 113
Sweet Potato Tart, 65
Tarte Tatin, 97
Terrine of Aubergine and Sweet Potato, 80
Tomato Mousse, 47
Tomatoes *Provençal*, 53
Vegetable *Gratin*, 111
Vegetable *Pâte*, 28
Vegetable Puree, 121